"An artist with the craftsmanship and g[...] omes along all too rarely. Such an artist with a stron[...] es and leads other artists—now that's really rare. M[...] as provoked and frequently moved by these reflection[...] ome unique refractions."

—PHILIP YANCEY, author of more than twenty books, including
Prayer: Does It Make Any Difference? and *What's So Amazing About Grace?*

"Like his art, Makoto Fujimura's essays harbor a depth of luminosity that requires and rewards patient contemplation. This collection is an important contribution to the conversation between faith and art and between art and our beautiful, broken world."

—ANDY CROUCH, editor, Christian Vision Project (*Christianity Today*);
author of *Culture Making: Recovering Our Creative Calling*

"At once bold and gracious, these 'despatches' from one of our finest living artists will provoke and inspire the reader at the deepest levels. If ever there were a time when we needed Fujimura's profound evocation of art as a harbinger of peace in a fractured world, this is it."

—JEREMY BEGBIE, Thomas A. Langford research professor of theology, Duke University

"William Blake wrote, 'They must always believe a lie, who see with, not through the eye.' Imagine the possibilities if the adverse of that statement were true. How profoundly could those who see 'through' the eye perceive the richness and depth of truth. Mako Fujimura has spent a lifetime of seeing 'through' the remarkable gift of his eye. He has painted for us, and now, remarkably, he has written for us about the truth he has seen."

—MICHAEL CARD, musician; author; teacher

"A bicultural abstractionist with a deeply meditative turn of mind, Makoto Fujimura has as much to say in words as he does in images. These essays, like his paintings, are rich and thoughtful explorations of art's redemptive power and its place in a violent, broken world. Rarely has a visual artist shed so bright a light on the wellsprings of his work."

—TERRY TEACHOUT, drama critic, *The Wall Street Journal*

"In the pages of this book, you will find the work of a man who loves the Creator of the universe and the art his creation produces. I recommend it."

—MARK JOSEPH, author of *Faith, God and Rock 'n' Roll*;
columnist, Foxnews.com and the *Huffington Post*

"Mako's art reaches from earth to heaven, and so does his poetic prose. His essays on the recent past bring out what a brilliant artist sees and a text-oriented historian might overlook: the texture, color, and poignancy of living in New York after 9/11 and viewing a world laden with both horror and hope."

—MARVIN OLASKY, editor-in-chief, *WORLD* magazine; provost, The King's College

"In these essays, Makoto Fujimura reveals himself to be an artist not only with pigments but also with words. His translucent prose warrants close, meditative reading to capture the subtle meanings refracted through its poetic lens."

—NANCY PEARCEY, author of *Total Truth: Liberating Christianity from Its Cultural Captivity*

"This elegantly penned collection sets a very high bar for future conversations about faith, art, and the hope we all have for the healing of our fractured world. Makoto Fujimura is a tender prophet of beauty and peace. The breadth of his spiritual vision is awe-inspiring."

—IAN MORGAN CRON, senior pastor, Trinity Church, Greenwich Connecticut; author of *Chasing Francis: A Pilgrim's Tale*

"Mako Fujimura's personal memoir circles on the demands of art and faith and their final inseparability. *Refractions* weaves a tale of art with the flames of 9/11 flickering in the background."

—DALE BROWN, director, the Buechner Institute, King College

"Mako Fujimura is about making peace. And he has long striven to make peace in his art and life. This arrangement of blogs, expansive in tone and urban in outlook, displays Fujimura's ability to find the transcendent in just about anything, from teaching a special-needs teen to wading through the ash-filled air of 9/11. It is an ability that makes him a joy to encounter, both in person and in his writing. His art—and his life—is about seeing and making connections in our world's conventions that most of us miss.

'Artists are at the margins of society,' he tells us, 'but they are like the Christmas shepherds, often the first to notice the miracles.' Fujimura represents a new breed of artists, whose lives match their work in their power to inspire. They remind us just how much we need them to notice the miracles."

—REVEREND SAM ANDREADES, pastor, Village Church, New York City

"These essays weave a luminous tapestry of observation and insight and they're a great read. Fujimura the artist has become a national treasure, and with these essays he demonstrates that he is also a serious writer and thinker. His prose is artful, moving, and bristling with wisdom."

—SCOT SHERMAN, director, San Francisco Theological Center

"In these remarkable essays—'refractions' indeed—Makoto Fujimura takes us unflinchingly into what he calls the war zone of the human heart, shedding light along the way on how art, fused with a hope born of a deep religious calling, transforms and redeems. Calling up such examples as Dante and Christo, T. S. Eliot and Warhol, C. S. Lewis and Leonardo, Fujimura writes of his personal struggle to make art and find meaning in a post–9/11 world. The result is a powerful and passionate exploration of what it means to be a Christian and an artist."

—ROBERT LOVE TAYLOR, author of *Blind Singer Joe's Blues*

"Expanding upon the writing of Kathleen Norris, Mako Fujimura brings together spiritual reflections on the observed world with the devotion of an accomplished painter to his work. Through lived encounters, Mako traces evidence of healing and signs of God's beauty and grace. Even in moments that seem to beg for closure, he pleads for a certain openness and wonder. And, offering us a glimpse inside his own art, Mako affirms every person's human capacity to create and serve."

—REVEREND SUSAN JOHNSON, Hyde Park Union Church, Chicago, Illinois

MAKOTO FUJIMURA

refractions

a journey of faith, art, and culture

NAVPRESS

Discipleship Inside Out™

NAVPRESS
Discipleship Inside Out™

NavPress is the publishing ministry of The Navigators, an international Christian organization and leader in personal spiritual development. NavPress is committed to helping people grow spiritually and enjoy lives of meaning and hope through personal and group resources that are biblically rooted, culturally relevant, and highly practical.

For a free catalog go to www.NavPress.com
or call 1.800.366.7788 in the United States or 1.800.839.4769 in Canada.

ISBN-13: 978-1-60006-301-5
Cover design by The DesignWorks Group, Charles Brock, www.thedesignworksgroup.com
Cover illustrations: Still Point – *Evening*, 2003; *Goldenfire*, 2006; *The Still Point-Love; Splendor Vision; Countenance Azurite E*
Author photo by Brad Guice

Some of the anecdotal illustrations in this book are true to life and are included with the permission of the persons involved. All other illustrations are composites of real situations, and any resemblance to people living or dead is coincidental.

Portions of *Refractions* have appeared in *Prism* (found at esa-online.org) and *World* magazines as regular columns.

"Come and See: Leonardo da Vinci's Philip in *The Last Supper*" was published in *Books and Culture* (November/December 2006, Vol. 12, No. 6, page 10).

"Planting Seedlings in Stone: Art in New York City" was published in *Comment* magazine, December 2, 2005.

"Fallen Towers and the Art of Tea" was published in *Image Journal*, no. 32 (Fall 2001).

All Scripture quotations in this publication are taken from the *Holy Bible: New International Version*® (NIV®). Copyright © 1973, 1978, 1984 by International Bible Society. Used by permission of Zondervan Publishing House. All rights reserved.

Fujimura, Makoto, 1960-
  Refractions : a journey of art, faith, and culture / Makoto Fujimura.
-- 1st ed.
     p. cm.
  Includes bibliographical references.
  ISBN 978-1-60006-301-5
  1. Fujimura, Makoto, 1960---Ethics. 2. Fujimura, Makoto, 1960---Religion. 3. Art and religion. I. Title.
  ND237.F79A35 2008
  759.13--dc22

                              2008030510

Printed in Canada

2 3 4 5 6 7 8 / 13 12 11 10

Contents

Foreword

The movie *Joyeux Noelle* (2005) is the true story of the famous "Christmas Truce" of 1914. It depicts how, during the hostilities of World War I, the French, Scottish, and German troops spontaneously laid down their weapons, came up out of their trenches, and fraternized during an informal, unauthorized armistice. And at the heart of this astonishing grassroots effort at peacemaking was art.

Kaiser Wilhelm II had sent thousands of Christmas trees to the front lines in order to boost the morale of the German troops. After the trees were set up over their trenches, in sight of the enemies' lines, a German soldier who was a tenor began to sing the Christmas hymn "Stille Nacht" ("Silent Night"). Soon the French and Scottish troops began singing along in their own languages. Finally, soldiers climbed out of their trenches without their weapons and began to talk, then exchanged gifts, and finally even engaged in games of soccer. (The full, true story is told by Stanley Weintraub in *Silent Night: The Story of the World War I Christmas Truce* (Plume, 2002).

The movie adds a fictional character to the true story in the form of a world-class soprano to go with the great tenor. The beauty of their singing breaks through the political dividing walls and unites the opponents in joy and tears. I've seen something of this unifying power even in my own church services. Because I minister in New York City, our congregation contains some of the best musicians in the world. The music in our services is always excellent, but occasionally we have a musical offering that is so superb and affecting that everyone listening is stunned into silence and moved to tears. And guess what? It is not members rather than visitors, or Christians rather than non-Christians, who are touched. Everyone is brought together; everyone is included. Interestingly, this happens only when the art is skillful and well-done. When the music is mediocre or bad, my members may be edified a bit if they know and love the musician personally, but visitors and strangers are bored and excluded by the experience.

Mako Fujimura is absolutely right to focus on the peace-crafting power of art. He quotes Tolstoy, who wrote that art *"should cause violence to be set aside."* It is our instinct toward freedom, justice, and beauty. This book of reflections explores Tolstoy's thesis with wisdom, humility, and grace.

I have been a friend and cominister in New York City with Mako since 1990. Mako's International Arts Movement has been a pioneering effort to integrate thoughtful faith with the creation of art that moves us toward the world "that ought to be." I'm delighted to see this book appear and honored to be able to recommend this book to all.

—TIM KELLER
New York City

Introduction

I write by the south window of my loft, three blocks from Ground Zero, New York City. The window overlooks the young sycamore trees planted on the opposite side of the street where one of the plane engines fell like a meteor, almost killing a pedestrian. Like that pedestrian, my family and I were spared from perishing that day, living so close to the site that will be marked as one of the emblems of a horror of the new century. And yet God has called us to call this our home.

God has taught me as an artist and a follower of Christ to live and work for the "prosperity of the city" (Jeremiah 29) in the ashes of September 11, 2001. Most Saturday mornings between 2003 and 2006, I sat down to reflect, or refract, on issues related to war and peace, but from the vantage point of an artist, a father, and a husband. As I wrote, I was admitting to the confusion, chaos, and deeper wrestling that I saw in my own heart during and after that fateful day.

In 2003 I was appointed by President Bush to the National Council on the Arts,[1] in recognition of my artistic accomplishments and my advocacy efforts via International Arts Movement.[2] Working with Dana Gioia, the superb poet and visionary head of the National Endowment for the Arts, I realized that we have to constantly labor to raise awareness for the arts in the United States and to present America via the arts to the rest of the world. I found that I had a particular vantage point from my bicultural upbringing to do so with some objectivity and passion, as well as with empathy of knowing that the world also suffers from trauma of one kind or another. My new responsibility to advocate for the arts in America increased my travel schedule. Thus, I wrote some of my "Saturday morning essays" during my travels, weaving in experiences from my international journeys. I remember trying to complete some of these essays by the frost of the plane window flying over Asia before the piercing deep blue of the night sky lured me to sleep.

Terry Teachout, the drama critic for the *Wall Street Journal*, who later joined the Council, encouraged me to keep writing in the blogosphere, saying, "Very few times in history do we have the opportunity to shape a new medium for communication. The blogosphere is one of those rare opportunities." My daughter, then thirteen, taught me how to post a blog with images, and I was ready to take on a new medium.

Here, then, are dispatches from various points on my journey of art, faith, and culture, written from the perspective of an artist living in twenty-first-century Ground Zero and wrestling with the issues of humanity. As a visual artist living and working in New York City, I also dwell in the multifaceted reality of the post-modern visual arts world, a multiphrenic world of shock, cynicism, and irony. I write from within that world, from the perspective of someone who loves to engage with and create art but also as a Christian whose central identity is in Christ, the ultimate Artist and Peacemaker.

Why art in a time of war? Jesus stated, "Blessed are the peacemakers, for they will be called sons of God" (Matthew 5:9). The Greek word for peacemakers is *eirene-poios*, which can be interpreted as "peace poets," suggesting that peace is a thing to be crafted or made. We need to seek ways to be not just "peacekeepers" but to be engaged "peacemakers." In such a definition, peace (or the Hebrew word *shalom*) is not simply an absence of war but a thriving of our lives, where God uses our creativity as a vehicle to create the world that ought to be. Art, and any creative expression of humanity, mediates in times of conflict and is often inexplicably tied to wars and conflicts.

Art can play a central role in the making of peace. Jim Hall, the legendary guitarist, in receiving the Jazz Masters Award, stated, "Jazz is our great peacemaker."[3] When jazz musicians travel around the world (they are more respected today outside of the U.S. than inside), their music carries a message of collaboration, the freedom of improvisation, and community — really, the fruits of democracy.[4] Jazz communicates beyond the barriers of politics and ideologies, as music speaks a universal language.

Leo Tolstoy, the Russian author of *War and Peace*, wrote in *What Is Art?*:

> The task of art is enormous. Through the influence of real art, aided by science, guided by religion, that peaceful co-operation of man which is now maintained by external means — by our law-courts, police, charitable institutions, factory inspection, and so forth, — should be obtained by man's free and joyous activity. Art should cause violence to be set aside.[5]

Art "should cause violence to be set aside" because to Tolstoy, who wrote under totalitarian oppression, art expresses the desire for, and instinct toward, freedom, justice, and beauty. Tolstoy's argument for this ideal for the arts continues: "The destiny of art in our time is to transmit from the realm of reason to the realm of feeling the truth."[6] In other words, the language of the arts translates the universal longing for peace into the tangible *experience* of the desire for peace. The arts provide us with language for mediating the broken relational and cultural divides: the arts can model for us how we need to value each person as created in the image of God.

This context of rehumanization provided via the arts is essential for communication of the good news. Jesus desires to create in us "the peace of God, which transcends all understanding" (Philippians 4:7), so that we can communicate the ultimate message of hope found in the gospel, the story of Jesus, who bridged the gap between God and humanity to a cynical, distrustful world. The arts provide a necessary backdrop for such an enduring conversation.

In my studio, I use ground minerals such as malachite and azurite, layering them to create prismatic refractions, or "visual jazz." Via my art I hope to create a mediated reality of beauty, hope, and reconciled relationships and cultures. As a founding elder of the Village Church,[7] I have found that mediation of any kind is never black-and-white but prismatic and complex too. In order to find hope, even in the midst of the broken and torn fragments of relationships, in order to begin to journey into the heart of the divide, we must first wrestle with the deeper issues of faith. We must be willing to be broken *ourselves* into prismatic shards by the Master Artist, God, so that Christ's light can be refracted in us.

Three months prior to September 11, 2001, I wrote the following for a Santa Fe art exhibit called Beauty Without Regret:

> Art cannot be divorced from faith, for to do so is to literally
> close our eyes to that beauty of the dying sun setting all around
> us. Every beauty also suffers. Death spreads all over our lives
> and therefore faith must be given to see through the darkness,
> to see through the beauty of "the valley of the shadow
> of death."
>
> Prayers are given, too, in the layers of broken, pulverized
> pigments. Beauty is in the brokenness, not in what we can
> conceive as the perfections, not in the "finished" images but
> in the incomplete gestures. Now, I await for my paintings to
> reveal themselves. Perhaps I will find myself rising through the
> ashes, through the beauty of such broken limitations.

Outside my window I see the young sycamores, once covered in the ashes of September 11, now turning to autumn hues casting their golden shadows on those passing by. Those who walk beneath the sycamore trees are of diverse cultures and backgrounds. Similarly, the culture at large is neither "Christian" nor "secular" but fantastically pluralistic, defying conventional categorizations. In each culture we will no doubt find evidences of trauma, like the ashes of Ground Zero, as we all find ourselves building upon our pulverized and fragmented past. We can choose to disengage from such intractable reality, as our hearts will struggle to find rest in such exilic ground as Hiroshima, Auschwitz, Darfur, Afghanistan, and so on. Or we can accept the splintered condition of culture as a kaleidoscope of common struggles, a reality that only the golden rays of God can restore and recreate via broken humanity. The latter is my starting premise in writing this book. As you journey with me in this refracted light, I pray the Spirit will indeed reveal God's presence in the undiscovered recesses of our creative journeys.

MAKOTO FUJIMURA
New York City, 2008

Columbine paintings being worked on in my New York studio.

I

A Second Wind

For years Dana Gioia served as a vice president of General Foods before leaving business to write full-time. He told me, "I would come home too late and very tired, but each night I made myself sit down at my desk and simply copy the last paragraph of the essay I was working on or the last stanza of a poem. Usually, I got my 'second wind.'" With this "second wind" he became one of the most prolific and influential American writers of our time. Many of his coworkers and employees did not even know that he wrote poems until he began winning significant poetry awards (leading to his American Book Award in 2001) and his essays began to appear regularly in the *Atlantic Monthly*.

I think of what Dana stated when I too find myself exhausted by my juggling act of trying to make ends meet, raising a family in this wild city. And yet, no matter how tired I am, when I prepare a panel with freshly spread handmade Japanese Kumohada paper and enter into the daily ritual of painting, I rediscover the joy of creating. The process of creating renews my spirit, and I find myself attuned to the details of life rather than being stressed by being overwhelmed. I find myself listening rather than shouting into the void. Creating art opens my heart to see and listen to the world around me, opening a new vista of experience. This is the gift of the "second wind." Such a state taps into what I now call eternal timefullness.[1]

A timeful experience is given when our minds are allowed to fully respond to the senses, to tap into the eternal reality that God opens for us via creativity. It's what William Blake, the eighteenth-century poet, meant when he wrote, "To see a world in a grain of sand, / And a heaven in a wild flower, / Hold infinity in the palm of your hand, / And eternity in an hour."[2] In order to "see a world in a grain of sand," we must pause to pay attention to the details of life, to let our eyes wander into the crevices of the earth below, to observe the shadows as well as the light, to perhaps even see how the light is refracted in the fragmental remains of sands. And such observational skills must be cultivated as a form of discipline, even in the midst of the hectic lives we lead.

I am often asked, "How do you juggle family, ministry, and your art all at the same time?" Many people have a hard time keeping their creative side alive in the busyness of our times. The advice I give is to dedicate a space, even a small desk, for working on nothing other than your art, whatever medium that may be. Guard against other parts of your life invading that dedicated space. Then, I advise them, do what Dana Gioia did: Make yourself sit down in front of that dedicated space. If you are a poet, like him, copy the last stanza you wrote; if you are a visual artist, open the sketchbook and look at what you have done. Most of the time, you will get your "second wind" as well.

Much of the days that I spend in the studio, I am preparing, waiting, and working to get ready to paint. Being a full-time artist means spending more than half of my time earning the right to create. I may be making a business call to a New York gallery or waiting in line at the bank to send funds to a Japanese papermaker. I could be simply stretching cotton canvas onto stretchers to prepare the surface or waiting for the paper to dry. Often, I am simply "showing up" to be in a regular rhythm of *being available* to create, and I may not feel creative at all. But my second wind kicks in to provide surprising moments of creative bursts. I value these moments, allowing me clarity and focus even in the midst of a stressful day.

An artist needs to be attuned to the nuances and subtleties of life in order to create. For me, this means paying attention to the materials I use. I need to know them in the same way that a writer would know, and love, his or her words. Thus, when

I open my jar of azurite to pour coarsely ground minerals into a white porcelain Japanese bowl and ladle in melted hide glue to mix, I begin to attune myself to another reality. The grains of sand being pushed about under my fingers begin to tap into the intuitive, creative core of my existence, but this arena also hungers for the sensual reality of earth underneath my fingers. Each grain of sand must be saturated with glue, which forms a protective surface that will act both as a binder and a form of varnish. So I am squeezing out the air in the process of mixing. But I am also squeezing out the unnecessary concerns of life, the intrusive voices that prevent me from focusing on the inner core. This daily ritual opens my senses to the reality of creativity. And my senses, soon engaged, propel me into a timeful journey again.

The minerals I use are like prisms, and they refract light more than just reflect it. The color spectrum and her subtle hues take a while to get used to, to truly see. The layering of these minerals reveals a mystery hidden beneath the surface reality, a world full of life and enchantment. It is a world not of competition but of complementation. In refracted light, no area is delineated as dark, or black; instead, the surface dances to the waves of light evenly. Refracted colors do not war against one another; they move in and out of our sensory arena, like an aurora extending her tails far into the horizon.

So today I pause and consider the world around me, from the May irises on Greenwich Street near my loft to the homeless man (Larry) around the corner from my studio. My role as an artist is never accomplished by executing a painting. My role begins there, but it extends into the earthy reality of the broken and beautiful world around me. Artist or not, when we begin to pay attention to the intuitive core of our experience and see the mysteries there, we too like Dana, will find our "second wind."

April 2004

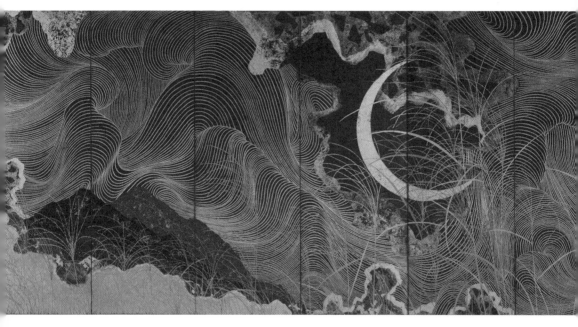

Matazo Kayama, *Hatsizuki*, 1967, 168.0 cm x 365.0 cm, Yugengaisha Kayama, Shin-seisaku Exhibit, #31.

II

Splendor

Nihonga (Japanese-style painting) master Matazo Kayama passed away in April of 2004. When I heard the news, I began a painting called *Splendor*, which was exhibited in his memory that fall in TriBeCa, New York City. I had studied under him during my graduate study years at Tokyo National University of Fine Arts and Music.

Professor Kayama (Kayama-sensei) selected me to be the first artist outside of their traditional curriculum in the prestigious post-MFA program, an arts doctorate program, an extension of lineage that has been in existence since fourteenth-century Japan. (I came in as an "outsider," an American with a Japanese Governmental Scholarship.) When I entered the university's Nihonga department, many luminaries of today's contemporary art were gathered there. Hiroshi Senju (who would later become my studio mate in New York City from 1994 to 2002) and Takashi Murakami (whom many consider to be the Andy Warhol, celebrated pop artist, of this day) studied there at the same time.

During this time in Japan, between 1987 and 1992, I had my formative spiritual transformation,[1] resulting in much deeper reflection and wrestling to integrate art and my newfound faith in Christ. Kayama-sensei, and others who oversaw me during that time, not only saw me adopt a new language of visual expression via Nihonga materials and technique but also observed my inner struggles with faith. When I entered the program, I considered art to be a sort of religion, one that required me to choose between allegiance to art and relationships. I wrote in my recent memoir *River Grace*:

> The problem that I could not overcome with Art being religion is that the more I focused on myself, the less I could find myself. A schism grew inside between who I wanted to be and what I did. I wanted to love my wife, but I saw, more and more, the distance between us. Art as self-expression became a wedge in our relationship. Meanwhile, every day, I sought higher transcendence through the extravagant materials. I found success in expression through Nihonga materials. And yet the very weight of beauty I saw in the materials began to crush my own heart. I could not justify the use of extravagance if I found my heart unable to contain their glory. The more I used them, the moodier and more restless I became. Finding beauty in nature and art, I did not have a "shelf" to place that beauty inside my heart.[2]

Before entering the department's doctorate lineage program, a student must complete four years of undergraduate studies and two years of master's. Then only two people are chosen per class to study under professors considered master Nihonga artists. At the time, Tokyo National University had two of "three pillars of Nihonga:"[3] Matazo Kayama, Ikuo Hirayama, and Kaii Higashiyama. For Kayama-sensei to take on a student outside of the traditionally closed inner circle, and one who was now identifying himself with Christ when the tradition was so closely tied to Buddhist and Shinto roots, must have been a radical decision; but he was himself a radical artist who found contemporary expression in the tradition of materials and visual language of seventeenth-century Japan.

Kayama-sensei began painting during World War II, eventually graduating from the same school I later attended. In countering his contemporaries' trend of advocating the injection of Western values into Nihonga, he instead took his inspiration from

Makoto Fujimura, *Splendor* (for M.K.) 66" x 89." Mineral Pigments, Gold Leaf on Kumohada paper.

the decorative screen tradition called Rimpa (seventeenth century). The Rimpa tradition combines decorative elements of patterns of nature into extravagantly rich images of gold, silver, mineral pigments, and sumi ink. Kayama's idiosyncratic works represent Japanese aesthetics today as they serve as a unique bridge to bring the tradition into modern Japan. He is, therefore, arguably the most important Japanese artist of the twentieth century.

During my trip to Japan, I wanted to pay homage to his legacy by visiting a special retrospective exhibit of his work at the Tokyo National Museum of Modern Art. I tracked his career from his early naturalistic works influenced by Bruegel[4] to his later paintings directly quoting Rimpa screens. He was also known for incorporating nudes into exotic metallic patterns, works that hearken back to his childhood days in Kyoto, where he watched his father, a Nishijin[5] master, design kimonos. As I was leaving Japan, I paid tribute to Kayama-sensei again, as there is an enormous public art commission that he completed at Narita Airport.

In Kayama-sensei's memoir *Infinite Space*, he writes this about silver and gold, which he calls "the third color":

> To me, gold and silver is the most mysterious of all the materi-
> als. Initially, I could not see the use of gold and silver in my
> works. . . . I considered it, foolishly enough, pre-modern and
> inappropriate for our present time. . . . So you might say, my
> view of gold and silver has changed drastically. Today, as I use
> considerable amount of gold, having mastered the material, I
> believe that such uses of traditional materials redefined my view
> of Nihonga. Uses of gold and silver, in both leaf and powder
> forms, allowed a development of my own Nihonga expression.[6]

When he gathered us students to teach us how to use gold, he had one of his assistants bring a clear piece of glass. He then proceeded to glue the gold right onto the glass. Lifting the glass, he showed us that the most pure gold is nearly transparent as it casts a bluish light and halo. I mentally pictured the new Jerusalem "coming down out of heaven from God, prepared as a bride beautifully dressed for her husband" (Revelation 21:2). The transparency of gold that Kayama-sensei was displaying overlapped with John's vision. For the new Jerusalem is a "city of pure gold, as pure as glass" (Revelation 21:18).

Therefore, when I was working on my Master's of Fine Arts thesis painting, *Twin Rivers of Tamagawa*,[7] I used the best gold possible (which meant more than one month's stipend would go into the painting) and layered it four times on one of the corners. I chose gold as a symbol of the City of God descending into our world, transforming earth and heaven, as described in Revelation 21. Kayama-sensei later selected this painting for the prestigious thesis purchase award and selected me as his only doctorate student for that year.

Kayama-sensei continues in his essay:

> The weight of gold and silver will capture even the passage of
> time herself. So one could find, within the visual space created
> by gold and silver, a moment of eternity.

In my mind, Kayama-sensei's vision for earthly materials began to tap into the greater reality of what Revelation passages describe: "The great street of the city was of pure gold, like transparent glass" (21:21). In other words, "the third color" would be based on transparencies of purity, layering of time and space that can be captured only with gold. It is remarkable to me that someone who does not share my faith can speak so clearly into the material reality of the City of God. But knowing Kayama-sensei with his insatiable curiosity, one should not be surprised by the audacity and the reach of his claims.

During his only exhibit in New York, Kayama-sensei was asked what he thought of the works that he saw in the United States as compared to Nihonga. He answered, I am sure, with a bit of the gentle swagger I remembered, his long hair accentuating his small stature, "For me, Nihonga is painting itself; it is the one and only pictorial form."

I think of this conviction as I sprinkle gold powder onto my *Splendor* painting. Kayama-sensei reinvented Japanese aesthetic into contemporary expression by deeply honoring and loving the past. He saw the Japanese notion of beauty as central to expression, not just for Japanese art but also as a universal principle for all expressions. If he saw the world via the lens of Nihonga, then I need to develop that same type of conviction in my newly found faith in Christ. I need to see cultures and expressions via the lens of faith, to boldly say, "For me, Christ is painting itself; it is the one and only pictorial form." Kayama-sensei's legacy, flowing out of Japanese aesthetic, is to me as clear as pure gold, handed to me by a great master.

May 2004

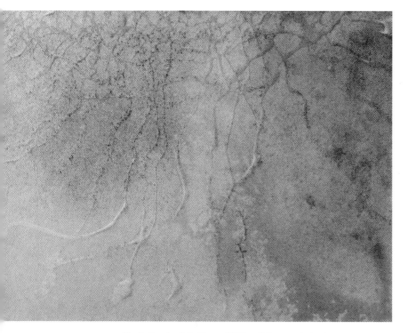

Net for Eternity, digital image of Makoto Fujimura painting in process,
collaboration with Corridor Press and Ryann Cooley, 2006.

III

Bert's Disappearing Weather Maps

Every morning Bert drew a weather map on the blackboard with his saliva. Carefully, he sketched out the exact weather map that he had seen the previous night in the news. I can see him now, tilting his head, limping slightly to the left as he moved, and drawing with his thick index finger. This act, seen by many of his teachers as a stubborn annoyance and by his psychiatrist as his "perseverant" activities, caused him to be part of my class at EastConn, a school in central Connecticut for challenged teenagers. These were students who could not be part of regular public school's special education programs. They were "special" special kids whom I had the privilege of teaching soon after I graduated from college in 1983.

Bert got into trouble not only for drawing on the blackboard but also for the mischief he created in class, for intentionally not following classroom rules. I realize now, many years later after having two teenage boys of my own, that his "rebellious" acts may have been typical. But in a special education setting, his antics became a "regressive behavior" that needed to be corrected. That, I was told, was my job: to control him somewhat.

When I met Bert for the first time, I doubted if any control would be possible. He had more facial hair than I did, was taller than I am, and was definitely stronger, despite his disfigured left hand. But when I introduced myself, he looked at me for a moment, as if to assess me, and then saw my name on the blackboard and began to try to pronounce my last name correctly. That act revealed the childlike curiosity that always resided deep beneath his greenish eyes. By the time the year was done, Bert was the only student in my class that would, and could, accurately spell my last name.

I noticed immediately, though, as I watched him draw on the blackboard, the detail to which Bert carried out his task. He had an acute visual memory but also the interpretive and expressive ability to take what he remembered into his own visual language. Even the "materials" he used had a direct connection with the content of the weather maps. "Spit evaporates," he muttered to himself, "and becomes part of the atmosphere." He then stood back to watch his mark disappear on the blackboard. To be sure, Bert was stubborn, but I recognized something else in him too. He was an artist, drawing to make a careful and diligent trace of his memory in a map and to somehow make sense of the world around him. As I watched his act every day, his ritual of evaporating drawing began to affect me.

"Hey, Bert," I said one day.

"Yees, Mr. Fu-ji-mu-ra," he replied in his bass voice, his eyes still childlike, despite his imposing stature and heavy workman's boots.

"How about we do a bulletin board project?"

"What would you want me to do?" he asked.

"Well, it's up to you, but we've got this whole bulletin board in the hallway filled with nothing very exciting. Why don't you do a mural of a weather map to start?"

Bert was amenable to this, although it did not mean that he would forgo his drawing on the blackboard first thing every morning. He took the markers I gave him, though, and enthusiastically worked on his colorful map. "No one's ever asked me to draw a weather map before in school," he said, snickering, immediately biting down on the cap of the marker with his mouth and twisting it open. "They just complained about it." I did get Bert to compromise on one thing though: He was to use a glass of water, rather than his spit, to create his morning ritual art on the blackboard. After I explained the possible health risks of eating chalk every day, he consented.

His maps, which took up the entire hallway and were redrawn several times during the course of the year, were filled with impressively accurate information on the current weather condition around the state. Bert had carefully studied the weather pattern in the papers. But his creativity took the raw materials of a newspaper weather map and made a kaleidoscope of colors into delightful patterns. Unfortunately, the unforgiving markers would cause him to be frustrated. He was not able to cover up mistakes. Half of the time, he would rip up the section he disliked, crumpling the paper and holding it under his gaunt, folded left arm, and I would find him back at the blackboard, watching his lines evaporate in the afternoon sun. The evaporating lines were certainly more forgiving, but perhaps he simply loved watching water disappear magically into the air more than making a permanent mark. The disappearing lines communicated in secret the intimate link between the visible and the invisible.

Now, some twenty years later, Bert's ritual seems closer to a spiritual experience than a "perseverant" activity. It was an act that tapped into healing, transcendent consciousness. I think about Bert as I watch my paintings dry in my studio. Recently, I started to make videos of my paintings drying as part of my exhibit. I increasingly find this act, as Bert did, to be healing. I watch the subtle movement of the surface of the water, and the watermarks made progressively as the piece dries; it stirs my heart to note details of life that we often take for granted. Beauty often resides in the peripheries of our lives. We walk past such humble miracles, such as the babe in the manger in a little village of Bethlehem, all the time. In the frantic pace of life, we need to slow down and simply observe natural forces around us and create out of that experience. What makes us truly human may not be how fast we are able to accomplish a task but what we experience fully, carefully, and quietly in the process.

Artists are often found at the margins of society, but they are, like the shepherds, often the first to notice the miracles taking place right in front of us. Since sensationalism, power, and wealth dominate our cultural imaginations, we may not be willing to journey to the ephemeral, as the Japanese poets of old have,[1] to see beauty in the disappearing lines or to see poetry in a drying puddle of water. The world seems to demand of us artist-types that we be able to explain and justify our actions, but often the power and mystery of art and life cannot be explained by normative words.

My art reaches for the heavenly reality via earthly materials. The intuitive core of my creativity, like the shepherds' hearts drawn to the birth of a Savior, simply desires to pay homage to the mystery of the moment. Lest we miss the birth of a Savior. Lest we fail to glimpse the glory of heaven hidden beneath the earth. The Spirit, though, can help to open all of our eyes to see the extraordinary in the ordinary, whether the material be extravagant minerals or a blackboard, whether we are watching an artist work or observing a special-needs child.

Bert ran off one day when I took the class for a walk in the park nearby. When he caught up to us near the entrance of the trail, I told him that I was upset and worried about him. "Don't worry, Mako," he said, "I have a map in my head, and so I am not going to get lost. Can't you trust me?" I wanted to yell at him as he lumbered back with me from the darkening woods, his boot laces untied as usual, covered now in spring mud. But another part of me wanted to embrace him. Yes, I did want to trust him, to see where his intricate map was to lead him, and to journey with him. There, artist to artist, we could draw and watch our created worlds disappear into the night. But I also knew that the society that would make Bert "useful" by giving him menial jobs after his graduation would not be as kind. We would have to account for our disappearance and always be required to justify our art.

July 2004

Golden Pine, installed at Oxford House, Taikoo Place, Hong Kong, Makoto
Fujimura, 198" x 270", Mineral Pigments, Gold on Kumohada.

IV

A Parable of Roots (Beijing Journal)

Due to my brother's wedding to a Chinese American bride, I had the opportunity to travel through China with my two boys. While in Hong Kong we visited my painting *Golden Pine*, an enormous commission at the Oxford House in Taikoo Place, the home of CNN/Time Warner. Consisting of nine ninety-inch by sixty-six-inch panels and over four thousand sheets of gold, *Golden Pine* is the largest painting I've ever done. We then traveled to Shenzhen, Kunming (a beautiful southwestern province), and then on to Beijing.

The press release about my painting read:

> In *Golden Pine*, Fujimura has created a site-specific work that
> interacts with and enhances its immediate physical environ-
> ment. The painting both echoes the reflection of the trees from
> the adjacent plaza in the massive glass wall at the base of the
> building and seems to produce a golden light of its own to
> respond to the late afternoon sun that illuminates it.
>
> In its aesthetic and material nature, *Golden Pine* also
> symbolizes the interaction of the traditions of the East and the

West. The artist is a first generation Japanese-American, born
in the United States, and has deep artistic roots in the West,
with a particular affinity for the more metaphysical aspects of
Abstract Expressionism and Color Field painting. Fujimura
has studied both in the U.S. and Japan, and this painting
technique has traveled from China to Japan, through him to
the States and now back to China in a thirteen century long
circuit. As a unique crossroads of cultures, Oxford House,
which is home to many multinational companies, is an ideal
venue for the master artpiece.

I was relieved to find the *Golden Pine* painting has done well in the public setting;
the minerals have settled well, and the layers of gold and silver have taken on the
transparency I desired. I intentionally exposed the silver on the bottom to allow it
to tarnish, creating a new sense of movement. The azurite now had a glowing quality, and it refracted quietly in the humid Hong Kong air.

As a first-time visitor to mainland China, I was stirred by the enormous flux of
culture, the tension between the old and the new. As a reaction to the Cultural
Revolution and the sociological impact from their "Ground Zero" of Tiananmen
Square in 1989, cities in China have become a capitalistic adventure, more like
Hong Kong. And yet, the sad result is that this remarkable feat of creating new
techno-savvy airports and city infrastructures, highways, and fancy malls is caus-
ing rapid inflation and a growing schism between the rich and the poor. Many
contemporary Chinese artists, such as Hai Bo (whose ghostly portrait work from
old photos dates back to precultural revolution days and were exhibited at Max
Protech Gallery in Chelsea), are expressing themselves from this divide, often
subverting technology to reveal the inner tension of progress and to disclose a longing to understand their community and ancestral roots in a new China.

What happens, then, in a country where premodern culture is thrust beyond
modernism and brought into the avant-garde of the twenty-first century? China
has always been identified as a culture built on ideological unity. Two of Beijing's
symbols, the Great Wall and the Forbidden City, now capture not only the country's
past glory but also her present tension. Like Communism, the Great Wall worked

to insulate her citizens from the outside. But now it attracts tourists worldwide, inviting people in rather than keeping them at a distance. The Forbidden City, the enormous golden Imperial city in Beijing, is now surrounded and dwarfed by new buildings of twenty-first-century progress. China is still a Forbidden City, and she flirts with visitors, inviting and distancing them at the same time. The tension is clear: The identity and the stronghold of Communism dominates China's past like the thick walls around the Forbidden City, and yet the sense of new nationalism grows ever more powerfully in the faces of Chinese people. Even as the past is boxed in, as the enormous walls desperately protect a museum of the past glory, the future grows ever more ominous as Beijing prepares to host the 2008 Olympics.

When I was finishing the *Golden Pine* in my studio in New York, one of the designers hired by Swire Properties[1] came in to observe. She noted that the bottom of the painting is exposed paper and that there is a subtle depiction of the roots of the pine trees, using Japanese sumi ink. The silver that is on the right bottom, tarnishing now a little, was also intended to create a separate space. The pine, a symbol of the longevity of culture, breathes in the golden air (a symbol of the City of God), but the

Tiananmen Square, 2004

bottom is of a different nature. My observer alluded to this and wondered out loud if the roots were not to be seen, giving dual significance to the painting, as in many Chinese paintings of pine trees.

Working intuitively as usual, I had not intended the divide between the bottom and top spaces to have any symbolic weight. My visual decisions are often based on many years of developing a visual language, and I do not attach symbolic significance to them. But now, having been to Beijing, I too wonder about the invisible reality of a soil underneath.

When Jesus relates the parable about a farmer sowing (Matthew 13:3-23), he tells us of the significance of roots. After my visit to China, I began to read this passage as one about cultural renewal. The farmer sows seeds (the "message of the kingdom"), and the seeds fall on three different types of soil. One type of soil receives the seeds gladly, but "since he has no root, he lasts only a short time." I now read this and think of Beijing. A "root" is directly linked to cultural conditions, cultural soil. Jesus implores us through this parable to pay attention to the roots growing underneath the ground, in places where we cannot see or observe. To do this requires attention beyond superficialities; it requires us to cultivate and nurture seeds. Just as it takes years for a pine tree to mature, the sower's job—whether the sower be an artist or a missionary—is more than just sowing but also discerning the soil.

China, for sure, is of rich soil. But the question that haunts me now is of the dual nature of the soil. On one hand is a country of enormous resources and curiosity; on the other is a country willing to systematically wipe out spiritual interest, imprisoning missionaries and spiritual leaders, thereby "cutting" the roots growing underneath. Like my painting, China has a dual reality.

The arts can tap into multiple irreconcilable realities at the same time, rooting deeply within the cultural soil. Artists often expose the tension between these competing points of view, but they also provide the potential to resolve various perspectives at the same time. But just like China, good art may raise more questions than provide simplistic answers. Good art can mediate deeply engaged dialogue that wrestles with the core issues of humanity. We need to pay attention to China and her arts of the new century, precisely because the multifarious conditions force us to ask deeper questions. Artists thrive on such conditions of exploration, often providing a surprising synthesis.

Just as the designer noted while looking at *Golden Pine*, the true question resides within the invisible reality of the roots underneath. Just as in the painting, the answer to this question is not revealed but hidden beneath China's layers. Breathing in the open air, as my Kumohada paper does, the soil is rich to those who are willing to consider China as a parable of the twenty-first century.

August 2004

From video by William Basinski.

V

The Disintegration Loops:
September 11th Issue

On September 11, 2001, musician and composer William Basinski peered over the East River from his loft in Williamsburg, Brooklyn, and watched in horror as the Twin Towers fell. He had been scheduled to interview for a job at the World Trade Center that morning. When I visited him a few days later, Billy told me that he had begun to lose his desire to continue to work, or even to continue to live, after that day. He, like many other artists, felt devastated by the experience. His heart was oppressed by fear and anxiety.

I prayed with him that day, and when I returned a few days later, he told me he had begun work on a series of compositions called the *Disintegration Loops*. I listened to the *Loops* with Billy while we looked at the footage of video he had taken of the sunset over the smoke of the fallen towers (see photo on opposite page). The sound of *Disintegration Loops* resonated and somehow completed itself in my mind. It affirmed an idea that came out of conversations I'd had with artists around my home and studio in what was now Ground Zero. As artists, we needed to gather our thoughts, pray, and reflect on what had happened.

"I thought I had been unwittingly commissioned to do the soundtrack for the end of the world," Billy would later recall at a gathering at The Village Church in Greenwich Village, commemorating the first anniversary of September 11. His melancholic composition *Disintegration Loops* played in the background.[1]

"I had recorded these bucolic, pastoral tape loops off the Muzak station in the early eighties and slowed them down a couple of speeds," Billy recalled, "but at the time they were too perfect and finished for me to do anything with." Some twenty years later, he rediscovered them in the process of archiving tapes at the end of their shelf life. "What I heard blew me away. Each one of the loops disintegrated in its own way, its own time, holding on to the end to what made it individual, and yet letting go of unimportant substance. I realized I had recorded the life and death of each of these melodies."

Finding himself numb to what he experienced on September 11, he heard the *Loops* he was working on in a different way. "I put the tapes back in to start editing them. Then I realized that the work felt like an elegy to the horror I just witnessed."

As he worked on the new composition, Billy also helped me to begin TriBeCa Temporary[2] in November of 2001 as a result of our prayers and conversations. TriBeCa Temporary ended up being over twenty exhibits, happenings, prayer meetings, and poetry readings until our closing exhibit in April of 2001. My studio mate, Hiroshi Senju, kindly contributed a small space, which Billy called our Ground Zero Tea House.

As Billy gave redemption to these loops, and as he helped in creating TriBeCa Temporary, he himself began to hear an echo of a greater redemptive grace. He began to hear the "still small voice" of God pointing him to eternal hope. He began to breathe in trust and dared to create again.

The release of the CD *Disintegration Loops* soon followed. It won numerous accolades and is now featured in National Public Radio's "Weekend America." One reviewer notes:

> There is another, eerier chapter to the story of the *Disintegration Loops*—that Basinski was listening to the playbacks of his transfers as the attacks of September 11th unfolded, and that

they became a sort of soundtrack to the horror that he and his friends witnessed from his rooftop in New York that day, a poignant theme for the cataclysmic editing of one of the world's most recognizable skylines.

The reviewer concludes, "The *Disintegration Loops* still wield an uncanny, affirming power. It's the kind of music that makes you believe there is a Heaven, and that this is what it must sound like."[3]

The reviewer, not knowing Billy's spiritual journey, still tapped into the core message of the *Disintegration Loops*. An artist's journey to believe in heaven can lead that artist to produce works mirroring that hope and can give others (including critics and journalists) the permission to speak of that redemptive possibility. Art has the capacity to challenge preset presumptions about what we believe, to operate in the gap between the church and the world, and to address deeply spiritual issues. The power of art is to convey powerful personal experiences in distilled language and memorialize them in a cogent manner. Such communication will resonate in the context of larger culture. The church needs to be involved in the arts and even advocate for those outside of faith, precisely because God has poured his grace in all of creation, and every artist, consciously or not, taps into the "groaning" of the Spirit.[4]

When I listen to the *Loops*, I experience once again the disorientation we all experienced on September 11. But through the very sound of disintegration, I also hear the refracting voices of eternity. Art offers the power to pause and the potential to find healing in the remembrance of things past. Art may be at times the only true memory we own in our experience of disintegration. Art may even point to a greater redemptive plan beyond "the life and death" of each of our melodies.

The Creator God has given us creativity and the arts so that we may "name" experiences, just as God commissioned Adam to name the animals in the Garden.[5] It is significant that God gave authority and freedom to Adam, "and whatever the man called each living creature, that was its name."[6] God did not question Adam's decisions. God completely entrusted to Adam the responsibility of naming as part of human stewardship over God's creation. In the fallen realities of our days, God continues to affirm our creative responses to the darkened horizon, and by naming the indescribable, we may yet rediscover our hope to endure yet another dark day.

God may allow our expressions to be etched in eternity, just as Adam's names were allowed to be the final word.

Just like the Muzak tapes, we are also disintegrating, but St. Paul reminds us, "Though outwardly we are wasting away, yet inwardly we are being renewed day by day."[7] Art taps into this work of the Spirit within while recognizing the honest depiction of our disfigurement. God, the greater Artist, will always seek to communicate via the disintegrating loops of our lives.

September 11, 2004

Genepic print by Kevin Clarke, who took rescue worker Mickey Flowers' photos and layered it with DNA patterns of survivors of 9/11. This print is a "portrait" of Ty Fujimura.

VI

Fallen Towers and the Art of Tea

"If I'd come out of school five seconds earlier," said my ten-year-old son C. J., when I finally found him, "I would have been in trouble."

He was covered in white dust, later called "dust of death," his hair speckled, his black backpack now gray. When Trade Tower One collapsed only four blocks away from C. J.'s school, firefighters pushed the children inside and shut the school doors.

The fireball of jet fuel incinerated thousands in a second and exploded a chain reaction of trucks and cars up Greenwich Street to the school. C. J. and his friends ran from one designated store to another, guided by teachers who told them to close their eyes. He almost ran into a tree, he said. It was a Japanese red maple tree planted in front of the schoolyard, a part of a garden and trees that he had helped to plant five years earlier.

The next morning, when my family returned to get essential items from our loft (now at Ground Zero), I walked by the tree, now covered in soot, each leaf sagging, coated in concrete dust.

On a summer night only a month before, I had sat with C. J. in front of his elementary school, P.S. 234, sharing a verse from Jeremiah 29. We looked at that red maple, the lights of the World Trade Center windows glowing above us in the evening haze. "Jeremiah told us to build houses and settle down and plant trees in Babylon," I said. "Do you think New York City is like Babylon or like Jerusalem?"

It was a lead-in question. The answer is *yes, like both*. In Jeremiah's day the Israelites were exiled from their identity as God's people, having forsaken God, and so neither the desolate Jerusalem nor the exilic land of Babylon held any promise for them. The false prophets spoke what people wanted to hear—it would be a short exile. But as a step of faith and a seed of restoration, God instructed Jeremiah to buy a field in Jerusalem, indicating that the battle would be long, even generational, much like what is going on now in New York City. "You helping to plant a tree, and being here with Daddy, moving into New York City," I said, "is being faithful in a foreign land. I suspect we have it much better than those Israelites, though."

My question to my son has become a lead-in question for me as well. New York City is like Babylon and Jerusalem at the same time, especially now. I survey the damage done to our "backyard." Three blocks away, the stadium lights set up to aid the recovery of bodies cast hallowing white light upon the rubble. Smoke rises like incense from the remains of the towers. Witnessing the devastation day by day, I have crossed the chasm of history, back to the fallen Jerusalem that Jeremiah witnessed. But New York is also the exilic land of Babylon in her pursuit of modern gods, such as wealth, fame, and cultural dominance, and how do I remain faithful here, even among the rubble? Reading the *New York Times* and then reading the Bible in the subway, I keep noticing a similar despair in the voices of the prophets of Babylon and in the newspaper's headlines.

"Until Tuesday, I was part of a ridiculously lucky generation," wrote artist Laurie Fendrich, a fellow parent at P.S. 234.

> For me, war was what I knew about from movies, reading,
> and my mother's loss, before my birth, of her brother in World
> War II. Now, like all Americans, I know something directly
> about war. I know it as a civilian, having been attacked here,
> in my own country, my own city, my own neighborhood.

> After Tuesday, I can no longer speak as a woman, or as an
> artist, or a New Yorker. Speaking in those ways — "speaking
> personally" — will no longer do. I have to learn how to speak as
> a citizen.[1]

Learning to speak a new language, whether as a citizen or as an exile, takes faith. We must trust in something larger than our experiences alone. And we must realize the error within us.

The Crowning Error

It has been said that we worship what our tallest buildings symbolize. Church spires defined city skylines in previous centuries. But they have been replaced by those "punch-card" towers, the pride of our progress.

The Twin Towers were the twin visions of technology and commerce flowing right out of modernism. On September 11, 2001, out of a cloudless, azure sky, right over the schoolyard, two airplanes cast sinister shadows upon our modern presumption, our trust in the twin vision.

The World Trade Center used to shade us at hot summer Little League games in Murray Street field nearby. They gave us respite, security. They stood for — and embodied — an economic system that we have come to depend on.

Postmodern art too was sustained by capitalism's nurture of modern technology and economy. Postmodernism depended on modern ideals that until September 11 were rarely challenged: build a higher, more impressive building; build a city that will surpass others in economic status and technological vision.

The arts require the same presumption, the same innocent belief in our power. Jeff Koons' pornographic sculptures and Andy Warhol's "iconic" pop art — postmodern art prospers by mocking the very hands that feed it, the hands of modern idols.

How crafty the terrorists who masterminded this catastrophe. Their "art," we must admit, was too powerful, too explosive, and thus all the more sensational. The terrorists accomplished in a single second what no art movement in a century could:

Their vengeance transcended and shattered the language of ironic distance. Takashi Murakami,[2] darling of 2001 Chelsea and the contemporary art world with his anime-based installations, stated, "The 'rules' and 'conventions' I learned over the years . . . have experienced a seismic shift. I must choose now whether to create in the chaos of 'new rules' or not."[3] Takashi and I attended the Tokyo National University of Fine Arts Nihonga Department together, and, even when we were students, we both felt that the conventional rules of tradition need constantly to be recalibrated to the present conditions. Whatever this "new rule" might be in a post-9/11 world, we need to at least admit to the seismic shift and begin considering the new reality.

For many artists I have spoken with, the fires of September 11 exposed the "rules" of postmodernism as irrelevant and narcissistic. Fendrich even calls for a type of restraint on art making: "Art and images need to be postponed. (I certainly can't think of painting right now.) We need, I think, to achieve intellectual control of our feelings, and direct our actions according to what is right and just, instead of to what pleases us as 'personal expression' or intrigues us as theory."[4]

But the real death knell for the twin symbols of modernism was not the insipid relativism of the postmodern agendas of our age. It began to toll long ago. The terrorists cleverly turned technology against its makers, injecting poison into the heart of modern idols, a poison of an ancient flavor, familiar to Adam and Eve. For in the garden, the devil also twisted what was given by God to be used for good by injecting terror into their hearts. It is a terror to doubt God's love and goodness. Terror eats away our innocence. But having swallowed the poison ourselves, we must remember that the flip side of fear is our own desire to enslave and to be in charge of our destiny.

F. Scott Fitzgerald wrote his lamentation *My Lost City* from the top of the Empire State Building in another dark autumn in 1931:

> From the ruins, lonely and inexplicable as the sphinx, rose the
> Empire State Building and, just as it had been a tradition of
> mine to climb to the Plaza Roof to take leave of the beauti-
> ful city, extending as far as eyes could reach, so now I went
> to the roof of the last and most magnificent of towers. Then I
> understood — everything was explained: I had discovered the

crowning error of the city, its Pandora's box. Full of vaunt-
ing pride the New Yorker had climbed here and seen with
dismay what he had never suspected, that the city was not the
endless succession of canyons that he had supposed, but that
it had limits — from the tallest structure he saw for the first
time that it faded out into the country on all sides, into an
expanse of green and blue that alone was limitless. And with
the awful realization that New York was a city after all and not
a universe, the whole shining edifice that he had reared in his
imagination came crashing to the ground.[5]

The crowning error of the city, pride, is in all of us. For the artist, as for Fitzgerald, cities represent both the height of our success and the depth of our failures. Both success and failure expose the error within, showing us that even the greatest city has limits. But the earthly city is not limited because of her boundaries. No, the earthly city is limited because her foundation is selfish ambition, the desire to control. We are all terrorists in that sense, attempting to twist God-given gifts to serve our greed and leaving Eden poisoned. Fitzgerald imagined falling towers long before the World Trade Centers were built.

Yet it would be a mistake to judge the city, to call it literally Babylon, to call what happened the judgment of God. Jesus told his disciples to repent when they saw the tower of Siloam collapse, rather than explain it away as God's judgment upon those who died.[6] In our own lives, no matter where we live, we have ground zeroes. Whether it be illnesses, loss of loved ones, or public calamities, our personal ground zero exposes our vulnerabilities and our fallenness, and sometimes even our own failures. Babylon and Jerusalem, the exilic and the destroyed, overlap in our cities and in our own hearts.

The Beauty of Metanoia

My studio is located ten blocks north from my loft. As I come home from my studio every day, I have to face south and walk toward Ground Zero. The Greek word for "repent," *metanoia*, means to turn 180 degrees around. In that sense, I am "repenting" every day. To walk toward the reminder of so many lives lost is to daily confront the evil that took place that day. The physical act of turning 180 degrees, doing this volitionally every day, began to link in my mind to the deeper repentance I needed in my own life, my own journey of faith.

During such a walk home, I thought of what my pastor had told me about another pastor who had lost his wife, his mother, and his daughter in a single automobile accident. Jerry Sittser began to see a particular nightmare over and over again. In this dream, he runs toward the sinking sun. He eventually becomes exhausted and collapses with the darkness enveloping around him. When he told his sister about this dream, she told him, "Jerry, you are running the wrong way. . . . If you turn around and run through the darkness, the sun will meet you on the other side."[7]

Developing a habit, a culture of repentance, will require us to walk straight toward the darkness, including our own imaginative power of vengeance. In the months after 9/11, many times as I walked home I began to hope for my own heart to forgive those who masterminded this catastrophe. As I did, I was reminded of how my sense of justice so easily leads to vengeance toward others. I was convicted of the terrorism in my own heart, of my desire to act out of vengeance and not out of love for my neighbors.

Our own acts of terrorism toward God drove Jesus to the cross. Jesus' slain body absorbed our anger and defiance, but more important, it absorbed God's just anger toward us. In that moment, all of what was most fair and beautiful in Christ became the hideous stench of a dying beast. Beauty was literally pulverized, destroyed, and the Eternal experienced the decay of death.

New York is, and has always been, full of idols. They are substitutions, created for the convenience of living a life without the reminder of our dependence on God. Material goods, appearance, personal comforts, family, and sex are all good gifts that we easily twist into our gods. These idols were exposed in our post-9/11 journey, at least in the hearts of those who are willing to turn to God. Of course, New Yorkers will choose to erect new idols or even rebuild old ones to cover up our dysfunctions. But my walk from my studio became a way to turn away from my own idolatrous heart, walk home to Ground Zero, and face a vacant reminder of our fallen nature and despair.

On one of those walks, I realized it is not enough to turn from our idols. *We must run toward the tower of Jesus,* which stands beyond and through our own ground zero experience. Jesus is the God of Ground Zero. Thus, God will turn our repentance into building blocks of the City of God, a vision of the New Jerusalem.

Surprised by Beauty (in Otego)

Late on the evening of September 12, 2001, my family and I drove north. Miraculously, we had been able to get our car out of our garage before it was shut down because of a gas leak. Even at the north end of Manhattan near the George Washington Bridge we could still smell the acrid smoke. We drove to Oneonta, New York, after dropping off a kind neighbor (a complete stranger before 9/11) and her dog on our way. She and her husband had welcomed us into their home that night so we wouldn't have to sleep in my TriBeCa studio. As I watched the smoke rise from another freshly fallen building, Number Seven, the series of lithographs I had been working on at Corridor Press became a welcome goal. My wife and I needed to keep the children away from the smoke and the calamity as much as possible.

At three a.m. on Interstate 81, thousands of stars lit up the sky, echoed below by the flags. The desolate highways brought back to my mind the ghost town of TriBeCa that morning, filled with the odor of death. In my head I still heard sirens shrieking in the bitter night and my own inept, feeble prayers uttered during my subway ride, trying to rush home.

Trapped in the subway for the forty minutes that changed the world, I had not even known that hell was breaking forth above me. All I had been able to see, finally having come out on Seventh Avenue at Fourteenth Street, was the smoke of the fallen towers. I had brushed against hundreds of evacuating businessmen and women as I ran toward my home, my studio. I saw again the blood-drained face of my wife, who met me at the studio, and experienced again the relief of hearing that all three of my children had been evacuated safely.

Shalom 19" x 24.75" an original lithograph printed by hand from stone on handmade Japanese kozo.

During the summer of 2001, at Corridor Press, master printer Tim Sheesley and I had been working on *Quince*, a series of lithographs of a medieval pear tree that I had sketched at the Cloisters. I had exhibited one lithograph as part of a triptych at Saint John the Divine's millennium Christmas celebration. On the morning of September 13, as I walked into the printing studio, noting the quiet of the turning leaves, I saw for the first time the pear tree images printed on thin Japanese paper (see *Shalom* image above). I had painted this as a test plate to get used to working on limestone again, and Tim thought the trial piece was successful enough to print.

As I pondered this simple image printed with silver ink, the work began to speak to me. It was like a small seed bursting into a joyous mess in my mind. I could almost hear it growing. I told my friends later that I heard the voice of Christ through the image. A voice of Shalom. I had not intended the piece to exist. But sometimes the Lord speaks through our peripheral expressions, like Mary's nard. That voice, like water, spoke out against the voice of fear within, the one that said, "What about the children now? What about our loft? Do you think it would be left standing? Do we dare move back into New York City?" But as I pondered the print, the whisper of Shalom became more real than even the tree itself.

I wrote in an e-mail to my friends:

> Create we must, and respond to this dark hour. The world needs artists who dedicate themselves to communicate the images of Shalom. Jesus is the Shalom. Shalom is not just the absence of war, but wholeness, healing and joy of fullness of humanity. We need to collaborate within our communities, to respond individually to give to the world our Shalom vision.

My studio mate, Hiroshi Senju, and I have had many conversations regarding what *shalom,* a biblical word, brings into the world. I had shared with Hiroshi the central place this concept plays in the writings of the prophet Isaiah and other biblical writers who longed for a reconciled world. Hiroshi was working on a historic commission for Daitoku-ji Temple in Kyoto, the birthplace of the Japanese art of tea. On September 11, as soon as I found my composure after gathering my family together, I wrapped all of the panels he had been working on, some thirty three-by-six-foot panels, to protect them from the smoke of the fallen towers.

Hiroshi called me from Japan and left a message on 9/11. He had been traveling, finalizing the plans for the commission at Daitoku-ji Temple. (His was among more than ten messages I received from Japan. The towers collapsed at 10:00 p.m. Tokyo time, while many in Japan were watching the news. Many stayed up through the night, concerned about us.)

"I realize that everything now has changed," said Hiroshi. "You now have a responsibility to minister and to heal. You have my support in this." In over fifteen years of friendship, this was the first time he had used the word *minister* to describe what I do.

Back in August, the two of us had decided to secure a smaller studio next door, partly to help Hiroshi complete the Daitoku-ji Temple commission. When he returned after 9/11, he told me that he wanted to take a break from the project.

"I cannot paint in the same way for a while . . . after looking at Ground Zero," he said.

We decided to make the studio a place where local artists could exhibit, dialogue, and find healing. We called it TriBeCa Temporary and dedicated it as an "oasis of collaboration by Ground Zero artists." I wanted to be sure that the history of Daitoku-ji, and therefore the history of the Japanese art of tea, would be woven into our efforts.

Sen no Rikyu, the sixteenth-century tea master who is most responsible for the development of the art of tea, lived and died at Daitoku-ji Temple in Kyoto. His teahouse still stands there. In China, tea was a form of celebration during banquets, but in Japan, Sen no Rikyu and others refined tea as a form of communication, and the teahouse as a minimal conceptual space. In a war-torn period of cultural flux, Daitoku-ji became the center of activity, and Sen no Rikyu became a new culture's main voice. I had told Hiroshi that summer that Rikyu epitomizes the meaning of *shalom.*

His teahouse had a distinctive entry called *nijiri-guchi,* built so small that a guest would have to bow and take off his sword in order to pass through it. It is no coincidence (but a historic fact ignored by most in Japan) that one of Rikyu's closest confidantes, one of his wives, was one of the first converts to Christianity under the efforts of Francis Xavier and others, the fruit of an influx of missionaries into Japan in the fifteenth and sixteenth centuries. Rikyu went with his wife to observe a Mass in Kyoto and there saw the Eucharist celebrated with a cup—Christ's blood—being passed around. This experience affirmed his vision for tea. His tea would be an art form: a form of communication equalizing any who took part, shogun or farmer, male or female. As a cup of green tea was passed, the teahouse would become a place of shalom. Five of Rikyu's seven closest disciples were Christians, later exiled by Shogun Hideyoshi, who gave power and prestige to Sen no Rikyu but later hardened his heart. To me, Rikyu redefined *art* as process-driven, integrated with life and peacemaking. To him, art played a significant role in everyday life or ordinary people; it challenged conventionality and the illusions of power.

Sen Gallery, my Tokyo exhibit in a typical teahouse.

Hideyoshi realized, quite correctly, that the egalitarian nature of tea would be dangerous to his power, and he became, by no coincidence, one of the greatest enemies of Christianity in history, ordering the execution of thousands of believers and closing Japan to foreigners for several centuries. He ordered Rikyu to commit seppuku, the most cruel art form of suicide, at the very teahouse of Shalom.

For my studio mate, who is a practitioner of tea as a modern artist often representing the Japanese aesthetic of today (he represented Japan at the Venice Biennale), bringing the ancient tradition into the present means finding innovation in today's context. He would, in fact, be exhibiting his eighty screens at the Asia Society and the Japan Society before they were installed at Daitoku-ji Temple in an exhibit called New Way of Tea. As a friend and a colleague, I would have the privilege of carrying this mission out as a "minister."

TriBeCa Temporary would be a small conceptual space, then, a Ground Zero teahouse. After six months of exhibits, performances, poetry readings, and prayer gatherings, we realized the dire need for such "safe" spaces for artists to struggle together, places not found readily in the arts community in New York City. Many artists commented on how liberating it was to exhibit their work, not based on agendas and commercial rules, but simply in vulnerability. In such a space, incomplete gestures were acceptable and even preferred. Perhaps being temporary and indefinable is the most honest statement that can be made about our post-9/11 expression. Such incomplete gestures must be made because the reality of the present darkness beckons us to respond.

I was able to secure, almost right away, the help of artists and writers such as James Elaine, curator and artist now at the Armand Hammer Museum in Los Angeles; composer William Basinski; critic Tiffany Bell; and Australian-born TriBeCa painter Denise Green, the last student of the abstract expressionist artist Mark Rothko.

But this effort also clarified a new definition of beauty and art in my mind. The Japanese ideogram for beauty is built with two Chinese characters, "sheep" (羊) and "great" (大). Apparently, in China, beauty was a "fat (great) sheep" (美). But in Japan, with the contribution of Sen no Rikyu and others, this word for beauty became refined and abstract. Beauty became associated with death and its sorrow. *Mono no aware,* a Japanese expression that captures the sentiment of sorrow (literally "sorrow of things"), points to the notion of beauty as sacrifice. In order for people to enjoy the feast at a banquet, a sheep must be sacrificed. Autumn leaves are most beautiful and bright as they are distressed with their impending death. The minerals I use in my paintings must be pulverized to bring out their true beauty. Art serves this kind of sacrificial beauty, and art should be redefined to consider the relational acts as much as products we produce to communicate.

In my many e-mails, I began to describe the courageous efforts of the rescuers on 9/11 as a "supreme act of beauty." Soon after, I received an e-mail from an owner of a contemporary gallery in Osaka, Japan. In agreement and encouragement, he quoted Dr. Tomonobu Imamichi, a professor of aesthetics at Tokyo University, and then later sent me the article that the professor had written for a philosophical journal. In it, Dr. Imamichi speaks of sacrificial beauty:

> In comparing beauty and goodness, I consider beauty to be the
> more transcendent of the two. The ideogram of "goodness" (善)
> is made up of two ideograms; one of a sacrificial "sheep" (羊)

on top of an ideogram of a "box." (口) To be good, it is only necessary to fulfill pre-determined (a "box") sacrifice determined by society. Paying taxes, or participating in traditions, rituals and such. The ideogram of "righteousness" (義) is made up of ideograms of sacrificial "Sheep" (羊) on top of "Self." (我) It means to carry the sacrifices yourself. But the ideogram of Beauty is made up of the sacrificial sheep on top of an ideogram for "Great" (大), which I infer to mean "greater sheep." It connotes a greater sacrifice, a sacrifice that cannot be boxed in by rituals or self. This greater sacrifice may require sacrifice of one's own life to save the lives of others. This sacrifice is not enforced by rules nor is it predetermined, but originates from self-initiative, a willing sacrifice. This is what is truly beautiful.[8]

Our call, individually and collectively, is to seek beauty and art through this kind of "greater sacrifice." The rescuers, along with other heroes of 9/11, redefined life's

true expression of beauty, which was forgotten by the "convoluted theory" of recent times. The firefighter's "art" was in their sacrifice. Their lives were offered up in response to the terrorist's "art" of vengeance in their "last extremity." Compared to the vengeance, those who sacrificed their own lives so that others could find life was the true *metanoia*, turning 180 degrees to face death head-on rather than fleeing. Through their example of sacrificial love, we can begin to know and experience true beauty.

TriBeCa Temporary Exhibit, April 2003. Collaboration with Albert Pedulla.

Homebound

We left Otego early on the Sunday morning of September 16, the car full of apples freshly picked by our children from the Sheesley's yard, and drove back to New York City. We needed to be back for what we thought to be a special time of mourning for our church, The Village Church. We found out that a few of our members had indeed escaped alive from the towers. A few, like us, had been displaced. None were lost.

On that Sunday, our son C. J. was to be confirmed as a full member of our church and to take his first Communion. It was to be his first public expression of faith. He had been meeting with our pastor throughout the summer in preparation for this day. We wanted to invite family members and friends to join us. We were planning to have a party for him. Now, the best we could hope for was to get to the service on time. I asked him, as I negotiated the hills of the Catskill Mountains, if he still wanted to go through with it. "Dad, I can't wait. I want to take Communion today."

After my fellow elders and our pastor prayed for C. J. to officially recognize him as a full communing member, he expressed his exuberance with a victory gesture I had seen him give after scoring a goal in soccer. Then, at Communion, he came up to me as I broke the bread to him, his hands cupped, and the voice of shalom filled my heart again.

"This is Christ's body, bread of heaven," I said to C. J.

If God can turn ordinary bread into a sacrament, God can turn anything into a sacrament. There is power of resurrection in this piece of bread going into the hands of a child. These hands, covered in September 11 dust last Tuesday, would be redeemed. God would take the very dust of death and turn it into life; he would turn twisted metal into a memorial of hope, and even the broken city of New York into the City of God.

Andras Visky, a Romanian playwright and scholar who was once imprisoned for his faith, told me that "without communion, there will be no community. Without communion, there will be no communication at all." Every time we break the Lord's bread and drink the wine, we affirm the foundation of Christ, who was shaken but not moved, broken but not destroyed. He is the "strong tower" we run to and find true refuge in, even as our own towers collapse all around us. This refuge, this communication, this community was what Sen no Rikyu desired, even though he was not a Christian, in his struggle to express humanity in a war-torn time.

With this Eucharistic foundation, we do not need to "postpone" art because art flows, for us, right out of that Table, from the very heart of our universe. If we center ourselves there, then we can go as far as the end of hell and still return home. We can even dare to have the innocence of a child in a world filled with fear and darkness. Jesus' command to not fear flows out of that Table as our promise toward true Shalom. At the table the Great Sheep still resides, inviting us to enter the Beautiful Gate through his suffering. No restraint is needed for the expression of hope in that morning light.[9]

November 2001

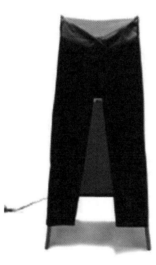

The Voting Booth Project: Where Art and Democracy Collide . . .
was exhibited at Parson's School of Design until November 15, 2004.

VII

Nagasaki Koi Voting Booth

The Voting Booth Project: Where Art and Democracy Collide . . . was the title of a benefit exhibit I had been invited to participate in at Parson's School of Design. Curator Chee Pearlman gathered fifty designers and artists to give each one an infamous portable voting booth from the 2000 presidential election in Florida (with chads still inside!) and asked us to do whatever we desired to transform it.

Being an apolitical artist, I was initially reluctant to partake, but after looking at the photo of the booth (strange, an awkward but intriguing device) and learning that the project was to benefit Declare Yourself, a bipartisan voter registration organization chaired by former presidents Gerald Ford and Jimmy Carter, I decided to participate.

When I received the booth and set it up, I was struck by both its simplicity and fragility. The voting booth came as an aluminum suitcase. Four folding legs unwound themselves to be attached in the bottom four corners. The blinders, which created privacy for voters, were then opened to attach to the edges of the suitcase. Sure enough, the chads were still there, gathering dust in the corners, a flimsy reminder of a historic election. I also noticed that the plastic enclosure that had held the voting cards reflected quietly from the dark enclosures of the booth. The florescent lamps, attached at the top of the booth, would have lit the punch cards as they were inserted, but in my booth the lamps did not work.

My art has been about precious materials refracting and about how that quiet emanation speaks to both our souls and eyes. But faced with this device, I had no idea how I would begin to create. I did not want to paint the voting booth, nor deal with it in some plastic terms.

For the *Splendor* exhibit at Kristen Frederickson Contemporary Art in New York City, I had been developing a language of refraction, as opposed to direct application of color theory or to seeing elements as competing pieces, into a video installation using a video I took in Nagasaki in December of 2003. It is a close-up of Japanese koi carp swimming in a pond near the site of the second atomic bomb explosion. To show the video, I had imbedded small television monitors in boat-like containers.

I decided to have a cloth cover for the booth and asked a friend, who had graduated from Parson's fashion school, to help. She was delighted to contribute to this effort and created a gray veil. The idea was to enclose the booth, to make it even more private. I wanted to place the small screen, with the images of koi, inside and let it reflect off the plastic enclosure of the all-important voting cards.

I wanted to create a sort of a prayer room, using images that reflected the enormity of individual decisions. When a *New York Times* reporter contacted me, I found myself trying to explain what I had decided to do.

"So you received the booth and set it up in your studio," she said, "and then what happened?"

"Well, I began to think about the privacy when we vote. I mean, we are all alone in there, in this darkness. We are supposed to cast a vote, which is a statement of a kind of faith, faith if not in a person, at least in a process of democracy."

I later thought how much like a confession the process of voting can be too. The issue of honesty, or integrity, is involved in making a decision, however polarized and imperfect the decision.

"It's a beautiful video that you installed . . . it is from Nagasaki?" the reporter continued. "Why Nagasaki?"

"I am a Ground Zero resident now, living three blocks from the towers, and after 9/11, I was troubled by the use of this term. I later realized that in a sense all of earth is 'ground zero' in that our failures and conflicts invade every aspect of our experience, leaving scars. Ever since that day, I have been dealing with this term in my work. I believe that artists can be agents for renewal and healing, that we can play a small part in rebuilding the world."

"So it's not a political piece . . . but you are one of the few conservatives—you're considered Republican, are you not?"

"Yes . . . but in my work, I try to go beyond the screaming matches of culture war. I want art to be a place of dialogue." I then e-mailed her an essay I wrote for the *Splendor* catalogue (partly because I felt so tongue-tied during the interview).

A few days later, in the *New York Times,* the reporter recaptured what I said:

> The only openly Republican participant, Makoto Fujimura,
> kept his political affiliation to himself in "Nagasaki Koi Voting
> Booth." Peering through a small slit in the dark fabric which
> covers the booth, viewers glimpse a video of multicolored
> Japanese carp swimming in a pool near the spot where atomic
> bombs fell on Nagasaki in 1945. "This piece is about history
> and tension and the issues we face today in this atomic age,"
> said Mr. Fujimura, who lives near ground zero in Manhattan.
> "I wanted to create a hopeful image, an image that wasn't
> sarcastic or even political but that reflects the private moment
> of voting. I consider it an almost spiritual event."[1]

I was surprised by the respect (despite her angle of needing to interview the only conservative chosen in the group of fifty artists) she'd given to what I said. Actually, she articulated what I said more succinctly than I could have surmised myself. I felt, as I always do in these newspaper interviews, forced to articulate what I had only began to understand intuitively. The reporter even gave me the last paragraph of a long article in which she quotes Christo,[2] David Rockwell,[3] and other luminaries. Evidently, I had a friendly interpreter this time.

We may feel just as awkward walking into a voting booth. The flimsy booth may damage our trust for the process of democracy, or in the future the uncertainty of untested devices may create concerns. But the process's lack of precision should not prevent us from casting a vote. Voting forces us to choose, to put closure to decisions we may have been vacillating about. By casting our vote, we put into motion a stamp of an intention of our hearts. No matter how perfect the voting machines may become in the future, the act of voting will always require a type of faith. This "faith," which may be a precursor to the greater and more lasting faith in God, reveals our vulnerability in our need to entrust others to carry our messages for us. Our small voices end up refracting into the swirl of a political and chaotic world. But even then, we may trust that these voices of privacy and, perhaps, our prayers for a better world can be registered. Even in the awkward and biased refractions of our intent, the core value of what we believe can still, somehow, be manifested.

November 2004

Illustration by RRP, Team Macarie

VIII

"L.I.B.E.S.K.I.N.D."

The P.S. (Public School) 234 gymnasium, which is two blocks from Ground Zero, was nearly empty when I entered to vote. This is the same gym where my children played basketball, the same gym where they waited for evacuation orders on September 11, 2001, three years ago. Except for a woman police officer and several volunteers, the space seemed unexpectedly vacuous, as I had in mind the long lines being formed in other parts of the country.

There was only one woman in front of me in the A–M line, and she tried several names before she had to move across the gym to the N–Z line. She had just gotten divorced, and her frustration could be felt in her silence as she moved away. As my turn approached, I put forward my driver's license before I stated my name. I've learned over time that "Fujimura" is better communicated by visible means, rather than audible. I helped the officials find my name in the black voting registration booklet and leaned forward to sign my name as the woman looked up at the next person in line.

"Libeskind . . . L,I,B,E,S —" I heard a voice say from behind me.

"Libe . . . what?" the woman asked. As Daniel Libeskind started to spell his name again, more slowly this time, I turned to face one of the most important architects of our time.

Daniel Libeskind was chosen over many other world-class architects vying for the design to replace the World Trade Towers. His design, which features a Freedom Tower soaring 1,776 feet up into the sky, seemed to me the most transcendent of all the design ideas submitted. Since the selection, the design process has been co-opted by a political process, with the owner of the towers bickering with local officials and Port Authority and Metropolitan Transportation Authority officials. Now, six major architects—Libeskind, Frank Gehry (who is designing the multi-arts complex), Santiago Calatrava (who is designing the World Trade Center Transportation Hub), David Childs (who was appointed by the leaseholder of the World Trade Center, Larry Silverstein, to work with the Libeskind design), and the design team of Michael Arad and Peter Walker—are trying to work together on the same site, although Libeskind's design and vision will still be the most visible and important aspect of the new skyline.

Photo of azurite rock by Ryann Cooley.
Used for my Splendor exhibit.

Small in stature, wearing long, square glasses and a black outfit, Libeskind smiled broadly as I introduced myself. I complimented him on the designs of crystal-like towers, which are now being built only a few blocks away from the school. I told him I am a local artist and gave him the invitation I happened to have in my pocket (artists: always carry your invitation cards!) for a current exhibit, also a few blocks away.

I told the poll workers that Libeskind is a very renowned architect and started to help them with his name. "You are an artist?" asked one of the workers, still quizzical, to Mr. Libeskind. He said, very kindly pointing to me, "No, but he is," and showed her my invitation card. He told me afterward outside the school that the design of the card fascinated the poll workers. I thanked him for his generous spirit, and as we parted, I noted how the fiery Japanese maple in the schoolyard was lit in the quiet light of this TriBeCa morning.

At a news conference in February of 2003, after his design was chosen for the site, Daniel Libeskind compared the "slurry walls" that surrounded the base of the towers to the resiliency of democracy. "The foundations withstood the unimaginable trauma of the destruction," he stated, "and stand as eloquent as the Constitution itself asserting the durability of Democracy and the value of individual life."[1]

On September 11, 2001, Daniel was in Berlin, preparing for the opening of his Jewish Museum Berlin after twelve years of planning and construction. He found himself on a trajectory of events that led him to submit a proposal for the Ground Zero design, despite the overwhelming odds against him. In our recent conversations, he told me that of the twelve architects invited to view the site to open the competition, he was the only one who took the invitation to walk about the pit of Ground Zero. "The other architects already had a design in their minds . . . actually I did too, but something happened at the pit."[2] In *Breaking Ground*, his book describing the process of designing the Ground Zero design, he writes:

> That is something I understood viscerally when I went down into the pit at Ground Zero with Nina; when I touched the slurry wall and placed my hand on its cool, rough face, it conveyed a text for what I had to do. In his *Confessions*, Saint Augustine tells of being in a state of despair. Then he hears a child's singsong voice. He doesn't know whether it is in his mind or real, but the voice keeps saying, "Take it and read it, Take it and read it." He interprets this as a divine command, and walks over to where he has left a book of scripture, opens it, and reads.[3]

He went on to write that as he looked up from the pit of Ground Zero to the other architects, he saw that they looked like ants standing at the edges of the site. "All of a sudden the memory of entering the New York harbor, at the age of thirteen, looking up at the Statue of Liberty came flooding into my mind."[4] Daniel's parents were Polish immigrants, Holocaust survivors who came to New York in 1959.

"I wasn't embarrassed by the nakedness of my emotions," he states; "I called my Berlin office from the pit and told them, 'scrap everything we've done for the site. . . . I have a vision for the crystal buildings.'"[5] He then went on to design the Freedom Tower, which he envisioned as being resplendent with light, to fill Ground Zero.

His vision for the site was heavily criticized by other power brokers as being too sentimental and idealistic. But Libeskind knew that the project required a personal touch that reflected the victims' faces. The public agreed. Libeskind's proposal "struck a common nerve," reported *The Wall Street Journal*.[6] But, on the day that the Master Design winner was announced, the *New York Times* reported, presumptively, that the other finalist, THINK group, had won the design competition. The design committee had chosen to ignore the public's opinion. The morning of the announcement, however, Governor Pataki and Mayor Bloomberg overruled the committee's decision, making Libeskind the final winner.

Just as in his previous major building, the Jewish Museum Berlin (which opened, by the way, on September 11, 2001), those who suffered in the atrocity would be his main theme. But he wanted to cast light into the dark crevices of Ground Zero, and he designed the space "so that it has no shadows on September 11 of each year from 8:46 a.m., when the first tower collapsed, to 10:28 a.m., when the second fell."[7] "The Wedge of Light" fills the site at precisely the times that the planes impacted the Twin Towers.

But Libeskind's overt patriotism continued to find resistance. Ensuing power struggles put the design, including "The Wedge of Light," into jeopardy. When I complained about the unfairness of the process during the interview I did for a British journal, he told me, "Architecture itself is a democratic art form. It's meant to be constantly reshaped by rigorous public and professional dialogue."[8]

Remarkably, *Breaking Ground* concludes with a chapter on faith, and quotes Hebrews 11:1:

> "Now faith is the substance of things hoped for, the evidence
> of things not seen." For an architect, these words are profound.
> We put our faith in things unseen each and every day. As
> I write this, there are designs of mine that may never be

built. . . . But I never give up hope; I always believe my buildings will be built, and given time, they almost always are. I am
enough of a realist to know that they may not stand forever,
although I build them to do so. What is more important to
me is that each of them captures and expresses the thoughts
and emotions that people feel. If designed well and right, these
seemingly hard and inert structures have the power to illumi-
nate, and even heal. You have to believe.[9]

The writer of the book of Hebrews speaks of this faith as a building block of the New Jerusalem and commends Abraham's faith in God as "he was looking forward to the city with foundations, whose architect and builder is God" (11:10). Elsewhere, Christ is called the "chief cornerstone" of the new holy temple and the new City of God (Ephesians 2:20). The Bible calls Christ followers to be both building blocks of the City of God and to be "expert builder[s]," or architects, of the new kingdom (1 Corinthians 3:10). We have much to learn from architects like Daniel Libeskind, who desires to create his designs in faith, in accordance with his Jewish tradition.

Art is an inherently hopeful act, an act that echoes the creativity of the Creator. Every time an architect imagines a new building, an artist envisions the first stroke of a brush on a white canvas, a poet seeks a resonant sound in words, or a choreographer weaves a pause in layers of movements, that act is done in hope; the creator reaches out in hope to call the world into that creation. And what if the creator reaches out to *the* Creator, the source and origin of creativity? Would not God be delighted? Even if no one else sees that offering, God alone can see. The treasures to be stored up in heaven (Matthew 6:20) can be our creative act done in faith. The Bible tells us the story of this creative God, who treasures his creatures, even as fallen and as desperate as we are. Jesus calls God "our Father in Heaven" (Matthew 6:9), and we are called God's children (Romans 8). The Bible tells us that God rejoices in our acts of creativity, just as any loving father would dote on his child's wild drawings.

Of course, we may twist that impulse and create art that does not reflect the Creator's genuine love. Everything we do, whether Christian or not, is tainted in some way by our brokenness, misplaced ambitions, and false devotions. We create edifices of selfish ego and frantically work to protect that idol. Even worse are those like the terrorists of 9/11 or the perpetrators of the Columbine High School massacre who create havoc by their destructive acts of hatred and vengeance. Theirs is an act of *anti-God*. They determine to rob, steal, and pillage lives, rather than to create in love and wait in hope. Anything not done in faith will always come back to haunt us. Thus Libeskind quotes Hebrews passages: "Without faith it is impossible to please God" (Hebrews 11:6). Libeskind, building in faith, counters that destructive force of 9/11 via his imagined hope: crystal buildings filled with light.

Despite our fallen nature, God desires to reflect goodness, beauty, and truth in us. God desires to refract his perfect light via the broken, prismatic shards of our lives. Art and creativity will end up being delivered back to the Creator's hands in that pure light. God's judgment of our works will then "reveal with fire" to "test the quality of each [person's] work" (1 Corinthians 3:13). God will even work via our imperfect works and will purify them to God's good purposes. Therefore, every day in my studio I endeavor to invite this holy fire into my life and my work, rather than to evade the light. I then wrestle against the encroaching darkness, to create in the same light that Daniel Libeskind imagines filling his buildings.

Thus that morning at the empty gym of P.S. 234, two creative artists with strange names did cast their votes two blocks away from Ground Zero. I was fortunate that both of our names were challenging to spell, thereby giving me enough time for a genuine conversation with an important architect and to eventually befriend him. No matter what the future holds, the voting process spells out the names of countless faces, one by one, and all votes will be counted equal after all. Perhaps, in that sense, it is good that the woman at the booth did not recognize us. Poll workers do not have to know who we are; they just have to identify our unique names in the black book, two artists trying, even with their votes, to honor those anonymous names etched in the slurry walls of democracy.

November 2004

Illustration by SPI, dbox

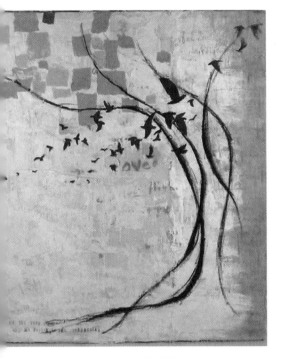

Christmas in Peace by Akiko Urakawa.

IX

A Beer Toast at Sato Museum, Tokyo

Mr. Harada, the organizer of the Considering Peace exhibit at the Sato Museum in Tokyo, Japan, surprised me with a suggestion: "How about if we close our exhibit on December 24, Christmas Eve?"

Considering Peace was a benefit exhibit of more than 120 artists, mostly from Japan, that I had initiated while planning for a Christmas exhibit at Takashimaya Gallery in Tokyo. Mr. Harada was one of my first collectors when I began my career in Japan in the 1980s. A fire chief turned cultural entrepreneur, he kindly agreed to become the project's chair. I and a few other New York and London–based artists participated as part of a greater effort called "Christmas in Peace." The works were donated and auctioned, and the benefit raised over $36,000 for United Nations Educational, Scientific and Cultural Organization (UNESCO) in order to help children in Afghanistan.

Since the majority of the artists were not Christians, we decided not to use the word *Christmas* in our titles. Those of us who were Christians wanted to, via art, experience Christmas in a new way by serving others in a foreign city, therefore removing ourselves from the context of overcommercialized frenzy we often find ourselves in. We wanted to "consider peace" ourselves.

So it came as a surprise to me when Harada-san suggested we close the exhibit on Christmas Eve, and I was almost incredulous when he kept on going with his requests. "What if we had candlelight? I mean, isn't that what you do on a Christmas Eve? Can we sing Christmas songs?" And then, using very polite, honorific words, he said, "We would be quite honored if you could speak about the true meaning of Christmas to us."

Despite the polite culture of Japan, a culture that honors guests from abroad, this request surprised me. But the project seemed to take on a life of its own. Artists began to arrive from all over Japan, not just to donate their works, but also to volunteer so that the museum staff would not be overwhelmed. We sensed there was much more than politeness at work.

Earlier that month, Mr. Kei Tatejima, the chief curator of the museum, had opened the artists' panel event, introducing the project this way: "This 'Considering Peace' was a collaborative effort bringing together unprecedented efforts from Japan, the US, and the UK. But I want you to know that the idea behind this is not just to raise money but to celebrate Christmas in a meaningful way."

Japanese public television covered the exhibit, and over 3.5 million viewers were introduced to artworks covering the walls of two floors of the museum. Apparently, an exhibit like this has never been done in a Japanese museum before. An art exhibit has never been used as a charity event in Japan. So unique was the effort that Mr. Tatejima had to inquire with government officials about the legality of the exhibit. They told him that though it was indeed unprecedented, it was legal to do so within certain guidelines. Then, there was a buzz among curators of other museums and galleries to follow suit. They wanted to know what the guidelines were so they could do similar exhibits. Many Japanese regional museums, built during the bubble economy of the late eighties, sit empty. The funding dried up after the bubble burst, and many museums now have no resources to buy paintings or even to mount a serious exhibit.

The art world in Japan, just as it is in New York, is in desperate need of a genuine community. If museums could be a place where artists and the public can come together to work to benefit the world, then even with limited funding they would benefit us all.

What inspired me most came from the mouths of the artists themselves.

"We do not have a forum to gather like this anymore. I find myself all alone in my studio. I realized that I needed a community like this more than I thought."

"I did not think that there was anything I could do to affect the world's grave situation. Thank you for giving me this opportunity. I was wrong to think that way."

We, the American artists, came to serve the Japanese, and they ended up serving us. They opened their lives and hearts to us, inviting us to their studios and homes. Via a small window of each individual piece, we saw a glimpse into how peacemaking is indeed a creative process. In these artists' sincere efforts to participate and to honor us, we had deep and meaningful dialogue that transcended our cultural and political differences. The creation of a "safe space" where we can agree to disagree is crucial in the creation of culture and community. Such a space, filled with the art of hospitality, invites us all to be artists of peace.

So, on Christmas Eve 2003, artists gathered at Sato Museum in Tokyo. There was quite a sumptuous spread of food. It was the first Christmas Eve party I experienced in which we started the evening with a beer toast. One of the artists arranged to have a huge Christmas cake (a Japanese tradition) made for the occasion. It had a Santa on top, skating in a pond of chocolate. After a singer-songwriter friend sang Christmas melodies, I shared the following about what I learned spending my Christmas season in Tokyo:

> A Japanese pastor wrote that the most important message of Christmas is that Jesus was born as a babe, weak and vulnerable to the world. A baby is utterly dependent on a mother and a father, and others helping the baby to survive. Imagine, one who would claim to be the all-powerful Creator in flesh, becoming vulnerable and DEPENDENT on fallen human beings like us!
>
> But when you think about it, a baby's strength also lies in this weakness, as he or she draws people together. The message of Christmas is a paradox. It is through the weak that power is displayed. It is through vulnerability that true, lasting security

is gained. It is through being utterly dependent on others that a true community is created.

The message of Christmas, then, can be applied to what we do as artists. What would our art look like if we truly believed that through our weaknesses, through even what we are ashamed of, we could create something that is lasting and meaningful, and incarnate hope back into the world? What if the power of a community is not in the display of power, but in the acknowledgment of our weaknesses? Artists can play an important role in helping a community to be authentic and honest. Japanese aesthetics already embraces the idea that weakness is beautiful: that what is wearing away and what is imperfect actually points to eternity.

I had my own epiphany in December 2002, while preparing for this project. I began to wonder if Japanese culture intrinsically longs for the true message of Christmas even more than our American culture. Less than 1 percent of the Japanese claim to be Christians. But the Japanese traditional culture affirms vulnerability and loss. Japanese poems and paintings from the Heian period (794–1185) are full of sorrow and sadness, and their poetic tradition of *mono no aware* can be literally translated "beauty in the pathos of things." The Japanese already recognize that, on this side of eternity, we must see the beauty in an empty cup.

As Americans, we immerse ourselves in our quest for individualism, and we champion material gains. We parade our "winners" and avoid being seen with the lowly "losers." We want heroes who are powerful and self-sufficient, and not someone who chooses to be vulnerable. In searching for dominance, we would walk right past that babe in the manger today. In fact, baby Jesus may be the opposite of what we desire as a culture to worship. We are quite undeserving of this gift, but Jesus came to us willingly. Among the messy, smelly, ordinary stenches, he became the candlelight in our dark, terror-filled world. He came knowing that he himself would be snuffed out, betrayed, and rejected by winners and losers alike.

Those who celebrate his birth know that this life is not the end of the story. Today, when we open this gift of grace, we are embraced by an eternal mystery. We open a gift of hope that breathes life into us, whispering that death is not the end. Such a message transcends our cultural blindness and any nationalistic biases.

Christ came so that we could fill the empty cup of sorrow with the wine (beer) of community and creativity. Christ came to fulfill a longing for beauty, a longing that the Japanese culture is already attuned to.

That evening in Tokyo, I was convinced that Jesus invited himself to be among artists who may not even know his name. (Jesus is known to have hosted some parties like this in his time). Some of these artists, I suspect, have already sensed his presence in their studios as they have labored to create peace via their paintings. All gifts of creativity, like the Magi's stars, point straight to a stable in Bethlehem.

One artist commented, "I never knew that Christmas Eve could be so meaningful and fun. . . . Why aren't we doing this every year?"

Why indeed.

Christmas 2004

Photo by Makoto Fujimura at Jose Limon dance rehearsal, 2008.

X

Dances for Life

I am absorbed in the magic of movement and light. Movement never lies. It is the magic of what I call the outer space of the imagination. There is a great deal of outer space, distant from our daily lives, where I feel our imagination wanders sometimes. It will find a planet or it will not find a planet, and that is what a dancer does.

Martha Graham, *Blood Memory*

On a balmy November day, I was privileged to attend the National Medal of the Arts and Humanities awards at the White House. Among the luminaries awarded were dancer Twyla Tharp, science fiction writer Ray Bradbury, writer Madeleine L'Engle (who, disappointingly, could not be present due to illness), opera composer Carlisle Floyd, and the remarkable architectural historian and teacher Vincent Scully.

The highlight of the day was to be able to congratulate in person the accomplishment of Twyla Tharp, who transformed modern dance with her revolutionary combination of classical discipline and ballet technique. Ms. Tharp noted that the last time she was at the White House was to accompany her mentor Martha Graham when she received the National Medal of the Arts in 1985 from President Reagan. I thanked Ms. Tharp for being present to receive the award, as I suspected that her political alliance would resist receiving such an honor from a Republican president. "Martha was not a Republican, either," she said, "but she received the award on behalf of other dancers. I receive this award in honor of her and of those to follow."

When I was briefly considered for the position of Chair of the Endowment two and a half years ago, I was interviewed by the assistant to the president in domestic affairs. I was escorted to the West Wing of the White House (which, unlike the spacious image from a television show, is cut up into small, cramped offices to accommodate many people), where I was interviewed by Margaret Spellings, later to become the education secretary. As I spoke to her, I found myself insistently advocating for dancers. She asked me why I was so passionate about dancers. "Martha Graham said that 'the dance is the mother of all the arts.' I know first-hand a dancer's struggle to continue their craft, which is so limited by time and physical demands."

But afterward, I did wonder too why I was so passionate about dancers. Perhaps it's because I cannot dance at all, and I have seen the tears of young dancers trying to make sense of why they continue to seek opportunities to dance, despite setbacks, injuries, and financial difficulties. Whether getting to know young dancers at my church, befriending a fellow parent at our children's public school who is a choreographer, or going to see Elizabeth Streb's brilliant, aggressively physical dance performances with my children, I have begun to experience the dancer's world in a different way. Dance, I began to realize, is the most extreme, distilled expression of the body, and it requires every aspect of human capacity — body, mind, and spirit — to produce. And yet it is the most lacking of funding and support.

When we watch dancers perform at the highest level, we are witnessing literal miracles unfolding in front of us. These dancers have bodies and abilities that can rival top athletes of any competitive sport. We are witnessing countless hours of rigorous training compressed into a moment of expression in a single leap; and then that expression is gone, and no photograph or video can capture the essence of that moment. You simply cannot buy, sell, or reproduce that singular action. Modern dance performers, especially, do not compete for medals or public attention, but they have given themselves entirely to make that leap, only so that a limited number of viewers can witness that physical calligraphy. Many of the top dancers I know willingly pay out of their own pockets to rehearse. They work in other jobs to sustain themselves and their craft; they sacrifice their youth to simply be on stage for a very limited career. No modern dancer goes into dance for fame or fortune. Dancers labor in love and without any fanfare or notoriety. Yet, despite the neglect, rarely do the dancers I know complain or grumble about their state. Their commitment and dedication inspires us but also reveals a great neglect.

There is something primal about dance that transcends all of the conventional concerns. Dancers embody the very ideal of the arts and fuse the spirit with the body. In other words, dance *incarnates*, and dancers bring this fusion in their bodies. God appeared in flesh via the babe in a manger, bridging eternal gaps in the incarnation: Flesh, therefore, is given the *weight of glory*.[1] God came, supped as a man, and bled to bring *our* bodies and spirits to merge into heaven. He defined humanity within his own body. As Dutch art historian Hans Rookmaaker famously stated, "Christ did not come to make us Christians . . . but that he came to redeem us that we might be human in the full sense of that word."[2] Our Lord humbled himself to have a body, to make himself vulnerable, to be lifted up in ignominy, and to find resurrection in that glorious body. A dancer, in a single leap, seems to hover in between the indescribable gap between time and space, taking us with him or her. By doing so, the dancer embodies our souls in the public arena, and perhaps that is the dancer's grand adventure.

Christians should be the first in line to see and applaud this fusion of body and soul. Christ is not an ideology, a sentiment, or a mental image, but a fusion of body and Spirit. Scripture speaks of how God turns our "wailing into dancing" (Psalm 30:11). Our bodies are not empty shells to be filled with souls but are mysterious and inexplicably tied to our redemption. Our Lord will dance with us in the coming age, and we should begin to prepare for that day.

Art is inevitably driven to our physicality, and both the potential and limitation of all of our craft will remain hidden in our bodies. In this fast techno culture in which engagement with the movements of our own bodies is restricted, we may be tempted to ignore such an age-old principle of our being. But I suspect that all artists will eventually return to explore the direct connection with the physical and ethereal. Ideas must be incarnated; ideals must be embodied. No matter how much technology allows us to aid fast and easy conveniences, we will always be drawn to that first love and first touch.

Theologian Calvin Seerveld, when asked in a conference what he thinks of technology, stated, "Well, we will always make love with our hands."[3] Love requires all of our physical senses. We will always desire to touch the babe in swaddling clothes too or be touched by him.

I suspect that, in celebration of those holy moments that can never be replaced by mechanical means, we will return to value the arts that honor the physical and again celebrate the "mother of the arts." Let us applaud those who so sacrificially give their energies, sinews, and bodies to the passion endowed to them. In that sense, dancers advocate for our whole humanity as they dance; we, by advocating for them, affirm the gift of physical grace, though limited by time and space, and witness for but a fleeting moment gravity defied.

December 2004

XI

Surfacing Dolphins

Last December, I had the pleasure of being invited as a visiting artist at Westmont College in sunny Santa Barbara, California. One morning, I got to take a walk along the beach, only a few minutes from a hotel filled with Charlie Chaplin posters. It does not take long to get seduced by the blissful scenery in this home of multimillionaires and legends of the arts (Martha Graham grew up there). One of the professors at the college told me to look out for dolphins swimming in the morning, and sure enough, a group of them frolicked in the blue-gray horizon.

As I interacted with students in the art department, I began to assimilate into the lives of youth and the limitations and potentials of a college environment. As I walked the beach, I began to ponder: *What, really, is art education?* I had in mind an earlier incident at one of the classes. A professor had encouraged students to bring out their best works to show me, and very few seemed bold enough to volunteer. So I suggested, "Bring out works that you don't like." In a few seconds, I had a portfolio of works that had been rejected in the students' minds as unworthy. We may all have a closet full of works that we are not proud of, works that need permission to come out.

We live in a culture of perfection, or at least in the superficial resemblance of things perfect. When we look at ourselves, we are trained by our culture to cover up our imperfections and blemishes. At school, or in life, we are driven to compete against others to refine and perfect our art. Yes, we need competition to excel, but if competition does not teach us humility, only shame, the business of education can create a culture of death. The best critique I have received in my life came from people who taught me who I was not, not just what I was good at. Failures teach us more than successes. Isn't education about giving us courage (the root of the word *encourage*) to take risks to fail?

James Elkins, a professor at the Art Institute of Chicago, wrote a book called *Why Art Cannot Be Taught*, in which he came to four conclusions:

1. The idea of teaching art is irreparably irrational. We do not teach because we do not know when or how we teach.

2. The project of teaching art is confused because we behave as if we were doing something more than teaching technique.

3. It does not make sense to propose programmatic changes in the way art is taught.

And quite blatantly:

4. It does not make sense to try to understand how art is taught.[1]

We make assumptions about teaching art, apparently, that are not justified by the very philosophy we have come to embrace in the art world. The postmodern art world has come to embrace, or at least acknowledge, that the basis of communication is no longer to be trusted. French philosopher Jacques Derrida argues in his "deconstruction" philosophy that the basic premise we accept to be true, including the notion of "good" versus "evil," cannot be trusted.[2] Language itself too is based on common cultural assumptions, and he went on to obfuscate such basis of meaning. Art, always influenced by philosophy, also began to question the traditional assumptions. Professor Elkins may simply be noting that the logical fallout of such questioning is being carried into the field of education. If every effort to communicate is fragmented, does it make sense to try to communicate at all? What are we pretending to teach, then? Aren't we sowing more confusion by pretending to teach while in such a fragmented state?

But as I walked the beach in Santa Barbara, one thing remained perfectly clear to me: *We depend on the light to see.* If we are drawn to the morning sun, we will always *have faith* to trust in the goodness of the experience of that light. If we do not, we would be better off to blind ourselves, or at least avoid the light, and stay in the darkness altogether. Similarly, art depends on the light to reveal the visual contours, our gestures, surface tensions, and shadows. Unlike languages, visual art is inherently dependent on the light to see. As such, any visual art assumes the same goodness of the experience of that light. Irrational or not, just as the dolphins so predictably visit the bay, we will just as predictably, often without thinking, come back to that light via our art.

But each step of seeing and responding to the morning light requires a kind of faith too. If we do not believe that paying attention to the world's "minute particulars"[3] would be beneficial, we would not ultimately spend time and effort to care to observe surface movements, grains of sand, nor frolicking dolphins. If we do not believe, or have *faith*, that such experiences have significance and meaning, we would not communicate that to our children. If we did not believe, or have *faith,* that learning is beneficial, we would not be in a school at all. In other words, it takes faith to teach art, and it takes faith to learn.

Education is a faith-based occupation: If we do not believe in the future of the child and the child's capacity to learn, to have faith in the child, why teach? And if the students did not believe in that future too why learn?

Since Westmont is a Christian college, I also began to consider what aspect of our biblical perspective permits us to explore the mystery of each teaching moment. Since I make assumptions that James Elkins chose not to make, and assumptions that our pluralistic colleges and universities would not assent to, I realized I was aided by the very "limitations" I have come to embrace. I can assume that such a thing as teaching is beneficial because I have been wooed by the Bible to have faith in the God who communicates and, as a result, to have faith in communication itself.

Our pluralistic society demands complex communication via various cultures and languages. If you have faith in a Creator who communicated via the pure media of stones etched with the Decalogue, then you can make assumptions about communication. For instance:

1. You can indeed speak and be understood.

2. What you hear is mediated by a benevolent mediator (the Holy Spirit) and not random echoes of an empty world.

3. There are laws that govern our relationships, and by accepting these boundaries, we communicate better.

4. It, then, *does* make sense to try to understand how art is taught because such effort will undergird our faith.

These presuppositions are what today's pluralistic society desperately looks for, but cannot fully embrace, in order to communicate to each other. These assumptions also give breathing room to *fail well*.

I have learned from Scripture to pay attention to works in my life of which I am not proud. They speak to teach me. I have learned that what the ancients called "repentance" is a journey of coming home to a place where all of our wretched works rest, but also where our wretchedness is overcome by light. This reality can powerfully alter how we view our lives and our art. Even our wretchedness cannot confine us, ultimately, or keep us from reaching across boundaries of cultures. But indeed our wretched state may be what draws us together.

But really, you might be asking, isn't this just your optimism and not your faith? Aren't you blind to the reality of our present condition? Perhaps, and it will be optimism and not faith if we cannot take failed works and learn from them. Blind optimism cannot truly teach because of the continuous denial of our failures. Faith is more honest. The honesty reveals our weakness but, at the same time, points us out of darkness into the light. That's what Scripture teaches us. Scripture teaches us grace. Our world does not. Therefore, art education that explicitly values biblical principles should go as far as to celebrate failures as much as successes. That should be the distinction.

Take, for example, *Sideways*, a movie full of Santa Barbara scenery. It is an ambivalent, brooding impasse of a movie but with a few poignant moments. The characters play out their frivolities to a typical irreligious fervor, noting along the way their obvious cynicism toward life. Just as professor Elkins continued to teach in art schools, despite his cynicism toward teaching, movie makers insist on making movies that celebrate how lost we really are in the light of the California sun.

Perhaps a pluralistic society breeds cynicism, or even a false, Sisyphean brand of optimism because so much needs to be overcome in communicating. Perhaps a "winner" today looks like a cynic celebrating in the light of a false Eden, drinking his pinot noir all alone. Watching this movie reminds me that acting, as teaching, assumes much based on the zeitgeist swimming about. I can only hope that a college environment can challenge such normative paradigms. We need to create an environment that can encourage even a cynic how to operate in a paradigm of a true, lasting desire, rather than continue to lie our way into fleeting desires. After all, how else can we entertain the presence of dolphins in our lives, playfully swimming in the refracting rays of Santa Barbara?

January 2005

Photo by Makoto Fujimura, copyright Christo and Jeanne-Claude, 2005.

XII

A Visual River of Gold

On a gray February Saturday morning, I headed out to experience the unfurling of Christo and Jeanne-Claude's *Gates* installation at Central Park. When I arrived at Columbus Circle, the thousands of orange gates (7,500 total) lined up in the walking path, greeting us. Before the unfurling, you could see through the gates like some op-art piece, each rectangle repeating itself, creating a visual echo. Through the winter trees the skies began to clear, with wispy cirrus clouds highlighting the evanescent sky.

The workers, wearing their gray vests signed by Christo and Jeanne-Claude, waited for the first moment of unfurling, all time coordinated via walkie-talkies and visual cues. Watching them work, I realized how much of this project must have been an extraordinary communal experience. Their excitement and dedication were palpable in how they moved together, stumbling through the details at times but definite in united hearts and enthusiasm.

Their cries of glee went up as the first of the gates was unfurled, the worker using a long pole to unzip the fabric, and the cardboard tube fell with a thud (the rolls were rather heavy, and they were warning each other to make sure no one got hurt with them). When the first one fell, I was standing but a few feet away, and the tube bounced with a loud *bonk* and startled me. But then, these *bonks* were heard echoing throughout the park, a call for the visual feast to begin.

"Wow, just like the drawings . . ." one of the workers mused as they continued to labor along the path.

Christo and Jeanne-Claude have done public projects for years, the most memorable ones being the pink surrounding of islands in Biscayne Bay, Miami, and the ghostly enveloping of the Reichstag, Berlin. They fund their own projects by selling lithographs and drawings, making sure that the art is free to be enjoyed by the public. These drawings are collage-like, overlapping photographs and charcoal drawings. I have admired Christo and Jeanne-Claude for their connectedness to the landscape and city drawings of twentieth-century post-war Europe and nineteenth-century Hudson River painters. But this morning, I could not but agree that the drawings themselves have the power to create reality before they happen. As part of their artistic vision, Christo and Jeanne-Claude impart expectation for the viewer to collaborate before the project takes place. And the actual transformative experience is in realization of that suspended belief crucial to their work.

The art of the early twenty first century may be remembered for its collective move from the inside of the studio to the outside. Andy Goldworthy, in his *Rivers and Tides* documentary, recounts how he began to create his works at the beach on the way to his art classes and realized that the world was his true "studio." Christo and Jeanne-Claude certainly paved the way for this paradigm shift. The most significant contribution of their works will be to help all of us believe that the world is the greater and more significant studio or stage and, more important, to see that our own creative vision can directly affect landscapes and cities. As the viewers journeyed through Central Park this February, we too can collaborate with Christo and Jeanne-Claude with our own desires and dreams. Just as the workers contributed so in synch, we too can collaborate with one of the greatest idealists/artists of our time, pausing to reflect how our ideals to create the world that ought to be might be realized.

I met Christo and Jeanne-Claude at a gallery opening in Ginza, Tokyo, during their installation of The Umbrella Project[1] in Japan. When I complimented Christo, he insisted on giving credit to his wife to make sure she was included as an equal partner. Born on the same day (he in Bulgaria and she in Casablanca) and later meeting in Paris, they live in a walk-up loft in Soho. Their affection for each other and their lifelong partnership in creativity seemed rather unusual in the ego-infested, greedy world of art.

They insist on not taking volunteers but on paying their workers, and for the *Gates* project they even paid for all the police overtime. They refuse to benefit from the proceeds of the sales of merchandise, desiring that their art be free from the consumer mentality that drives the art world today. An exile from a former Soviet bloc country, Christo seems always to be a consummate utopian, and Jeanne-Claude is his greatest champion. Perhaps the greatest ideals that they uphold are the belief in their partnership in life and their hope for a pure collaboration and communion with the public.

Christo called this offering "a visual river of gold." As I was meditating on this idea of "gates," I learned that the Scriptures use the word *gates* 111 times and *gate* 222 times. Revelation passages speak of many pearly gates on top of the golden streets of New Jerusalem. The City of God will apparently be a visual river of gold. I am reminded of my mentor, Matazo Kayama (see page 19), pasting a gold leaf upon a classroom window, telling us that "good gold, without much silver, is ever so transparent, and true pure gold is liquid." It's important to note here that pure gold is liquid and not solid. We will be walking through gates, literally walking on a river of gold. On that day, metaphors will be replaced by the density of reality, the vision of hope unfurled into a true and lasting city. These orange gates, therefore, seem to me to symbolize a cultural and spiritual passage from a solitary life to living in community, from devastation to restoration.

When Christo and Jeanne-Claude first imagined the project twenty-six years ago, Central Park, once so magnificently envisioned by Calvert Vaux and Frederick Law Olmsted, was a place of crime infestation and dilapidation. Though, I am sure, the artists will insist that there is no singular purpose attached to the gates, we can surmise that Christo and Jeanne-Claude's utopian ideals cannot let one of the greatest miracles of city design, called Central Park, sit idly in devastation.

At the completion of the unfurling, as the workers passed out swatches of the saffron fabric to eager partakers of this art-communion, Christo and Jeanne-Claude's utopian ideals sowed seeds of imagination into us all, all ready to tackle the next project, wherever and whenever that may be.

February 2005

XIII

Finding Neverland

From *The Terminal* to *The Polar Express*, old-fashioned innocence is back in Hollywood, winking her magical charm into our lives this year. But this charm seems most evanescent in Miramax's *Finding Neverland*, which I happened to catch recently en route to Osaka, Japan, for an exhibit at Yoshiaki Inoue Gallery.

Finding Neverland casts Johnny Depp (as James Barrie, the Scottish playwright of *Peter Pan*) and Kate Winslet (dying mother of four children, including Peter) in a tender look at James Barrie's life and offers a background (apparently fictional) account of the creation of Peter Pan in 1905. It offers rich reflection into the nature of creativity, an artist's struggle to incarnate his hopes, and an admirable exploration into the very nature of belief. Neverland is a place, if believed, all can enter into.

"Believe in what?" you might ask. These latest Hollywood movies seem to want to convince us to believe in something and the world would be a better place (remember *The Polar Express* with Santa's deep, resonant voice?). These movies pit children's innocent beliefs against our adult cynicism — "If you don't believe, you can't really meet Santa or get to Neverland."

But we may want to reverse that question to ask, Where does the desire to believe in belief come from? That's the imaginative landscape that *Finding Neverland* really invites us into. (By the way, if you ever doubted Johnny Depp's or Kate Winslet's ability to act with great depth and to incarnate that tension between cynicism and hope in a most serious manner, the movie greatly encourages a new assessment.) You see, good art does move us to believe in the possibility of belief, whether in ultimate reality or wanting simply to have hope in desperate circumstances. One Japanese commentator noted, "Though the actual historical evidence does not line up to the story told, this only goes to show how much a movie, any movie, is suspended belief in movie-making itself. *Neverland*, the movie, is indeed the true Neverland to be believed in."[1]

In the movie John Barrie invites twenty-five orphans into the theatre for *Peter Pan*'s opening. The play's financier, played by Dustin Hoffman, becomes irritated as Barrie has the children sit next to Edwardian arts patrons. The children's innocent laughter as Peter Pan is unveiled brings life into these initial tense moments. Their wonderment as they see Peter Pan fly across the stage moves the respectable gentlemen to begin to be children once again. Believing, which Barrie insists to be most necessary for the children's health and growth, must be incarnated into action. Neither this movie nor the character of John Barrie would be convincing apart from his own wrestling with this question and actually being torn by the gap between his own vision and the reality of survival, while also fully experiencing the cruelty of death. In that brokenness Barrie's own heart is moved to sacrifice his freedom to commitment, embracing the orphans into his own theatre of life.

The Greek word in the New Testament for "believe" is *pisteuo*, which suggests belief not as a sheer intellectual exercise of having "blind faith" or to imagine and will us into irrational faith but belief as a relational axis of trust. Good acting and good art moves one to this place of trust. What inspires us, after all, is not being force-fed to believe in belief itself but to be moved to desire belief and expose our deep need for trust in each other. That *pisteuo* compels us to a greater sacrifice for each other. *Neverland* brings us effectively to that place, to create a shelf for such a longing for a greater love. In that place, orphans are always welcomed into our imaginative enterprises, shocking us out of our conventional comfort zones.

Now, if a movie can communicate all of this via the ten-inch screen of a United Airlines flight from Newark to Osaka and woo this weary traveler to land in Japan with joy and delight, that movie must be deemed successful. The word *entertainment*, after all, originally meant "giving rest to the weary,"[2] or even hosting strangers into your home to nourish them. If Hollywood can begin to truly do this, we would be no worse off than that. It might even feed our orphaned souls, waiting for hope, waiting for Neverland.

March 2005

Photo by Makoto Fujimura, paper maker at work in Imadate, Japan.

XIV

Cloud Skin

I recently visited the town of Imadate, a premier papermaking town in western Japan. As I arrived in the local train station, freshly fallen snow highlighted the thatched roofs of traditional houses. Nestled in between the mountains of western Japan, the town in Fukui prefecture has an ideal combination of cold, pure water and fibers of mulberry plants and *totoro-aoi* (a type of hibiscus plant used to facilitate mixing the fibers), the materials and conditions needed to create paper of remarkable strength and durability. Known also as the temporary home of Murasaki-shikibu, the world's first woman novelist (*The Tales of Genji*), the town itself seems to still glow with a thousand years of Japanese tradition.

Other traditions make individual layers of paper and then paste them together. Japanese papers (washi) are unique among the world's papers, as layers of paper are woven all together. This technique of weaving fibers together allowed Heisaburo Hirano in the early twentieth century to create the largest handmade washi paper available anywhere, almost canvas-like in thickness and strength, called Kumohada Mashi, or Cloud Skin paper. I have used Cloud Skin paper up to sixteen square feet.

The Japanese government still uses washi and sumi (calligraphy ink) to record their proceedings because of the paper's durability. Washi paper is far more durable than canvas because the weavings are tighter and fewer air pockets exist. Of course, all paper is vulnerable to puncture. But in a sense, paper's vulnerability is her strength. Therein lies the essence of Japanese culture and beauty. When fibers of mulberry, hemp, and other natural fibers are woven together, these weak materials become most durable and permanent. These papers are also meant to breathe with the surrounding air, the air itself acting as the best cleanser to keep the paper healthy.

The Japanese realized a long time ago that nothing is permanent. Therefore, it is better to respect the aging process, to value the ephemeral over apparent permanence of materials. The age-old concept of wabi (poverty) and sabi (rusting away) insists that what is truly beautiful is not the permanence of things but the impermanence of things, that a culture is not just the product of culture but the knowledge of a craft that is passed down from generation to generation.

I was encouraged to see, therefore, that there were many young men and women who had begun to apprentice at the papermaking town. Many had gone to art schools and had learned the art of Nihonga (Japanese-style painting), only to realize that part of their learning art was to understand firsthand the process of making paper.

The Japanese government, surprisingly, does not have a system of supporting and funding traditional crafts and art forms. Being on the Council on the National Endowment for the Arts has opened my eyes to how we are able to fund many art forms that find their protection in our country. Our National Heritage Awards, given out in the fall of every year, honor those masters of crafts from all over the world. Can it be that America has a better understanding of how we need to protect the world's cultural forms and voices because our diversity breeds our interest to shelter traditions? Do we see more objectively, perhaps, having been exiled from our cultures, what makes our own traditions unique and valued? I now find myself trying to convince the Japanese how valuable and beautiful their culture and traditions are.

What the Japanese do so well is to develop an art form in collaboration between nature and art. We can indeed all learn from the Japanese how the stewardship of culture is directly related to the stewardship of nature. If, for instance, by pollution and overbuilding we lose the resources that make these fibers, and if the pure mountain streams are tainted, we can no longer sustain papermaking. But the Japanese seem to have found a vision to take care of their resources well and by doing so are nourishing their country's tradition and expression. And yet, even here, the tradition lives its tenuous life, with many of the papermakers around the country not being able to continue with their craft. By continuing to use these natural materials, I too collaborate with nature. My visit was specifically to create a dyed paper that could be used with gold, as in my recently exhibited piece *Splendor Gold*.

I found out recently that the Declaration of Independence is written on the same type of paper as the Kumohada paper I use. Imagine that: Our democracy is literally written out on delicate rag paper. As we pay homage to the signatures that began the great experiment, we might ponder the symbolic significance of the material. The form suits her content; democracy too is vulnerable to puncture, as on that beautiful azure day of September 11. But on the other hand, our democratic ideals are also resilient because democracy is allowed to breathe with the changing air of the times. The strength and durability of democracy are not in the permanence of ideologies but in the wrestling of ideas in the process of collaboration.

The ecosystem of a democratic culture, like these mountains of western Japan, should allow for diverse cultural expression to thrive in collaboration. This ecosystem is worth sustaining because it is through these expressions that we will find a common language of longing for beauty and delight in God's world. As I paced the premises of the papermakers, smelling the sweet aroma of fibers being boiled and stirred, my thoughts were stirred in a curious blend of cultural fibers and identities; my creative journey too is being woven in layers by master papermakers.

May 2005

Gretchen Bender's *Butterflies*. Photo by Ed Gorn.

XV

Gretchen's Butterflies

The Kitchen, a black-box theatre located in Chelsea, Manhattan, a catalyst for much of the experimental art and music in recent times, was packed with renowned artists, critics, and avant-garde art lovers. But we were not there to perform, or begin an innovative program, but for a memorial service.

Gretchen Bender, an artist friend, had passed away at the age of fifty-three, to the shock of her friends and colleagues who came to honor her on that cold January day. Many influential figures of the art world, such as Cindy Sherman, the premier photo artist of the last decade; Robert Longo, whose seminal *Men in Cities*, a series of drawings of frenetic, dancing bodies captured the art world of the 1980s (one of the famed drawings featured Gretchen); and Elizabeth Streb, the MacArthur award winner in progressive dance, were all present.

Gretchen's sister, Valerie Godwin, whose husband, Clyde, was the former pastor of my church, introduced me to Gretchen in 1999. Gretchen then graciously took part in my TriBeCa Temporary project, which I curated after September 11, 2001.

Gretchen was a pioneer of the emerging media art phenomena in the eighties. Yet, as *New York Times* critic Roberta Smith wrote in her obituary, she remained in the background. She was part of "the generation of early 1980s Pictures Artists. . . . Combining aspects of Conceptual Art and Pop Art, these artists used the images of popular culture to dissect its powerful codes, especially regarding gender and sexuality." Many credit her today with pioneering "the rapid-fire hyperediting now pervasive in film, television, and video art."[1]

Gretchen's accomplishments range from PBS documentaries to museum retrospectives. But what continues to be etched in my mind is her public work of 1990s collaboration with Miran Fukuda in the Tameike-Sanno subway station in Tokyo. The Tameike-Sanno collaboration appropriated, ironically, the images of the World Trade Towers. When I visited Gretchen's studio, located in South Street Seaport near Ground Zero, she told me of her experience after 9/11:

> I was sitting on the steps in front of my studio, reading an article in a newspaper about the "butterflies" the Russians had dropped all over Afghanistan in the last war, and I looked up from the paper and stared blankly as I tried to comprehend the meaning of the article: what kind of cruelty was it that children picked up these "butterflies" floating down and were blown apart. A sense of general despair for the world began to creep into my whole being when, suddenly, two feet in front of me, a REAL butterfly floated by my face. I couldn't move in astonishment. I had never seen a butterfly in all my years on South Street, and it was November, and it was Ground Zero air quality, and where did this fragile emanation appear from? All those souls lifting out of the white dust, off the collapsed shards — a sacrifice, a gift, a hope, for a spiritual shift in the world.

She then created an installation for TriBeCa Temporary that became a highlight of our six-month effort to "create an oasis of collaboration for Ground Zero artists." She folded hundreds of white origami butterflies and carefully arranged them on the floor, representing her experience that, she repeatedly told me, was her "resurrection moment."

Then she told me something remarkable: "I could never do this in Chelsea galleries or museums." I asked her why. She answered, "Well, it's too tender and beautiful."

At the memorial, one of her friends reminded me that this was the last work she ever exhibited.

It was evident to those who attended the memorial service how much Gretchen struggled with the hype, the greed, and the backstabbing that characterizes the art world. She was too sensitive, too vulnerable, too unguarded. During the service, her longtime partner talked about how he had written pages and pages about how the art world had destroyed her, but then decided to restrain his comments. He nevertheless wanted to convey how she was victimized and swallowed up by the vicious realities of the art world and felt betrayed. But perhaps he did not have to share the details in his notes.

The service started to take on a confessional tone; one after another, emotive artists recalled Gretchen's delicate nature and gave account of their personal struggles in their relationships with her and with each other. I suspect that the language used was too brutally honest for some. One of my friends commented afterward, "I've never heard so many four-letter words at a memorial service!"

Bill T. Jones opened the memorial service by singing an old spiritual as he stepped out from the audience. He slowly walked down the stairs and moved onto the main stage. His body swayed; his feet began to tap.

Then, one of Gretchen's assistants stood to play a tape of a song that Gretchen used to listen to in her studio on her tape player. The worn-out tape is by an underground artist I'd never heard before called Daniel Johnston,[2] but the assistant said, "It's from 1 Corinthians 13 in the Bible." I was surprised, as I knew how much Gretchen struggled with the church and Christianity. And yet when the song started to play, almost everyone in the room knew the tune, except, ironically, those of us who were Christians. We knew the words well, but not the tune. "Love is patient and kind, love is not jealous or boastful. It is not arrogant or rude. Love does not insist on its own way. . . . Love never ends."

Perhaps Gretchen herself was "too tender and beautiful" for the art world after all. Perhaps she saw herself in that butterfly, a lone specter of a strange mystery in terrible, dark days. Where would a creative butterfly like Gretchen migrate? Would the art world continue to alienate and divide in our Darwinian grasp for a flash of spotlight? Would we then miss the small "resurrection moments" of our ordinary days? Gretchen, at last, saw the butterfly. Perhaps we would miss it or ignore it, even if the butterfly flew in front of our own eyes. Perhaps what the artists present wanted to acknowledge on that cold day in January was the reality of how far we have fallen short of our own expectations and, even, our desires.

If Elaine Scarry, who teaches at Harvard University, is correct, true beauty forces us to admit our own errors. She notes:

> The beautiful, almost without any effort of our own, acquaints
> us with the mental event of conviction, and so pleasurable a
> mental state is this that ever afterwards one is willing to labor,
> struggle, wrestle with the world to locate enduring sources of
> conviction — to locate what is true.[3]

Though, as a neoplatonic thinker, she would not directly link this experience of beauty with biblical principles, her instincts to bring the issues of beauty and the issues of justice to advocate for beauty stand out in today's academia as unusual, or even brave. In the high academia and the arts circles of the 1990s *beauty* was a taboo word. Astonishingly, Dr. Scarry points out that art and beauty have the potential to lead us to confession of sorts, to "admit our errors."

Gretchen *saw* the butterfly. She experienced beauty and then began to experience a "spiritual shift." Perhaps, in missing Gretchen, will we artists admit the vulnerability and unguarded innocence of a true artistic experience? Will we, the church, allow a community of broken, brutally honest, creative people lead the way for admission of our errors? If so, then the culture at large can espouse a deeper and authentic confessional experience, giving it permission to have a powerful experience of forgiveness and healing. It can even start by our truly *seeing* a wayward butterfly.

That day, the small, avant-garde theatre in Chelsea, for but a fleeting moment, became a communal confessional box, filling it with hymns and spiritual songs.

What I have learned as an artist living in New York City for over a decade is that what happens here, in avant-garde theatres and the arts, will eventually filter out, affecting the formation of future cultural products. What is celebrated in Hollywood, Madison Avenue advertisements, fashion walkways in Paris, and popular music heard in Starbucks today had their seedlings in unknown avant-garde artists of over a decade ago. That is why it is so crucial to have the church's mediating presence in culture, especially in what is known as the avant-garde arenas.

As I left The Kitchen (only to return a few months later to do a collaboration called, ironically, *Shangri-La*), I felt certain of Jesus' presence in the room. As the author and fulfillment of that song by Daniel Johnston, Jesus would have invited himself there, as the manifestation of the "unknown, rejected" singer of a worn-out tape of old. And there, his "dancing has turned to mourning" (Lamentations 5:15). At that moment, he would certainly have been unguarded and perhaps as vulnerable as a single monarch flying in the ashes of 9/11.

June 2005

Little Gidding, photo by Makoto Fujimura of a work in progress, 2008. Mineral Pigments on Kumohada paper.

XVI

Why Art?

The aim of art is to represent not the outward appearance of things,
but their inward significance.

Aristotle

As an artist, I often find myself trying to answer the question, "Why art?" Why is art necessary in our lives and in our education? How can I justify investing so much of my time and expenses in being an artist and in helping others by advocating for their artistic expressions? Why do we need the arts in our local communities?

I could begin to answer these questions by pointing out that we now have a lot of research pointing to the economic benefit of bringing art into communities. We also have efforts to scientifically prove that the arts help us directly in education, in improving children's school grades, and in helping them to engage better with their worlds. We are hopeful that in a few years we will have several reports that give hard data to the positive effects of the arts to aid in education, giving data to what we all recognize anecdotally. We already have evidence that the arts help slow down dementia and reduce stress and give great benefit to the lives of the elderly.

But usually, in these gatherings for advocacy of the arts, I end up listening to people. I want to know what deeply matters to them. And I often find that art is already present in the areas that they are most engaged in and most passionate about. The man I may be speaking with may not know anything about art in New York, but he may talk about his child's dream to become a dancer or an actor. Or about a movie that affected him deeply. He may speak of his business enterprises and may point out that businesses are starting to realize that the "bottom line" is not really sufficient; there is a "second bottom line," or a third. Business schools are now inviting designers to discuss creativity and design and are beginning to apply these principles into business practices because workers are no longer content to work in bottom-line-driven companies. They want their whole person affirmed, and they want community. What I hear these workers stating is that they want their humanity back. And in that conversation, art always presents itself as an expression of humanity.

I was recently speaking at a church in New York, and I asked the congregation what they enjoy doing on Sundays apart from going to church. Everything they listed had something to do with the arts and entertainment. Art is everywhere, from the food we order in restaurants, to the clothes we purchase, to paintings hanging in museums. Aristotle defined the arts as "our capacity to make." So, we could broaden our discussion into medicine and the sciences. Even if we do not include these sister disciplines in our conversation, one thing is for sure: Our cultural productions and our art will define us, whether we like it or not. *Art expresses who we are.*

One of my most frustrating moments as an arts advocate was seeing the Janet Jackson Super Bowl halftime fiasco, knowing that the show was being broadcast in China for the very first time. What do the Chinese think of us now? We in the United States have come to define ourselves by how we degrade ourselves, and we have exported that vision to the world.

When I traveled with The First Lady to represent the United States at the UNESCO general assembly several years ago,[1] one of the UNESCO officials told us of her fears in America's reengagement with UNESCO: "We are struggling to believe that the U.S. can bring more than McDonald's, Coca-Cola, or Hollywood movies." (I might add pornography to that list, but she was too polite.) We tried to convince her and other UNESCO leaders that we have a very unique patronage system that encourages democratic patronage of the arts, such as the National Endowment for the Arts and the National Endowment for the Humanities. But when the official connected NEA projects with the Shakespeare in American Communities program, the Jazz Masters program, and the touring of Martha Graham dance troops, she became convinced that we were committed to a higher vision. These distinctively American forms of art, I would argue, are the greatest fruits of our democracy. And we have every reason to celebrate and broadcast with pride what freedom has brought us.

Tolstoy stated, "Art is not a pleasure, a solace, or an amusement; art is great matter. Art is an organ of human life, transmitting man's reasonable perception into feeling."[2]

Art is a building block of civilization. A civilization that does not value its artistic expressions is a civilization that does not value itself. These tangible artistic expressions help us to understand ourselves. The arts teach us to respect both the diversity of our communities and the strength of our traditions. I encourage people not to segment art into an "extra" sphere of life or to see art as mere decorations. Why? Because art is everywhere and has already taken root in our lives.

Therefore, the question is not so much "why art?" but "which art?" In other words, our worlds are filled with art that we have already chosen for our walls, our iPods, and our bookshelves. We become patrons of the arts by going to see movies, plays, and concerts or by watching television. We are presented with a choice, and this choice is a responsibility of cultural stewardship. Just as we have responsibility for natural resources, so do we have responsibility to be stewards of our culture.

What, then, does the current cultural ecosystem look like? NEA research, such as Reading at Risk, is pointing to a cultural epidemic of disengagement. We are reading less and less; but even more problematic, in my mind, is how we are less engaged with civic activities, with nature, and even with sports!

The Columbine High School incident and 9/11 taught us that we can use our imagination either to destroy lives or to save lives. At Columbine we had on the one hand a girl in the library reading *Macbeth* (she wanted to be an actress) who experienced a recent conversion to God, and on the other, a teen pointing a gun at her head, asking her, "Do you still believe in God?" and shooting her. Cassie Bernall's[3] diary shows a girl struggling with similar issues as the perpetrators, and yet she chose to embrace faith, rather than to embrace nihilism. The account of her transformation inspired countless others to express that belief. Her killer's actions prompted others to copy his destructive acts of horror.

On 9/11 we had on the one hand militant hijackers who turned their imaginative vengeance into determined evil acts. On the other hand were firefighters who climbed the falling towers. We have to realize that before any of these terrorist acts were committed, they were imagined. We swim in the ecosystem of imagined actions. We are responsible for how we respond to that power. We do have a choice between saving lives and destroying lives.

If we do not teach our children, and ourselves, that what we imagine and how we design the world can make a difference, the culture of cynicism will do that for us. If we do not infuse creativity, if we do not take the initiative to help our children imagine better neighborhoods and cities, despair will ruin their imaginative capacities and turn them into destructive forces. These are the lessons of Columbine and 9/11.

I get to spend my days thinking and imagining, painting and writing. I think about my journey, which started when I was a child simply wanting to draw and express. I had encouraging parents, and I am blessed with a wife who suffers alongside me. The life of an artist is never easy, but I take it seriously because I know that imagination has consequences.

But I do on occasion go back to that question, "why art?" because it was a question I addressed to myself in a diary for a creative writing class in college many years ago. My professor wrote back in his comments, "Your questions are valuable, and I encourage you to push that question further, as many of the writers and artists have done in the past: Why live?"

Perhaps that's why we need the arts. By continuing to create and imagine a better world, we live. We have no alternative today. The path of apathy, the path of cynicism, and the path of the terrorists have incarnated their realities in our backyards. To have hope is no longer an optimist's escapism — it is the only path to the future.

Originally presented as a speech July 2005 in Leesburg, Florida

John James Audubon, *Pileated Woodpeckers*, Dover
edition photos. Pileated Woodpeckers are often
mistaken for the Ivory Billed Woodpeckers. Ivory
Billed Woodpeckers are rarely recorded or painted.

Optimal Foraging Theory: Can You Have Your Birds and Eat Them Too?

On the day that the *Arkansas Democrat* reported the sighting of thought-to-be-extinct ivory-billed woodpeckers, I was touring the Tyson Foods kill factory in Springdale, Arkansas, where two hundred thousand Cornish hens are eviscerated each day. I'd been invited as part of a group to experience the inner workings of this Fortune 500 company, whose CEO is now a committed Christian. Tyson, the largest producer of protein products in the world, has indeed been going through a major change in recent years and is now known to be a faith-friendly company. The tension of living out one's faith in the workplace seems to swirl within the greater tension that exists between stewardship of natural resources and capitalistic interests. It seemed an ironic coincidence that we'd be visiting this factory on the same day that the newspapers reported this remarkable sighting of woodpeckers that many still believe to be extinct.

Upon entering the factory, wearing hairnets, smocks, and florescent earplugs, we saw small hens hung by their legs on a silver conveyer harness, parading in front of us with mind-numbing efficiency. The steamy yellow odor, mixed with bleach, enveloped us. Every thirty minutes, the tour guide told us, the workers rotate positions as a way of keeping them engaged in their tasks—a result of recent changes.

He went on to tell us that a decade ago, the turnover rate for the workers was close to 100 percent annually, but now, after the reforms, the rate is close to 30 percent. The workers, apparently, are finding the changes amenable and finding opportunities within the company to advance.

There was one room, though, where we spotted only a few workers. It was the "zero point," where the birds are captured, hung, and plucked with laser beams and increasing automation with each step. The hardest manual task, as it turns out, is actually catching the birds, several of them at once, and then hooking them onto the conveyer belt. Everything else is automated, including the actual point of death. As I watched the birds one by one approach the "zero point" of a laser beam aimed at their necks, there was an eerie silence; the weight of life hung heavily in the dark room.

We were also introduced to some of the workers. Half were migrants (legal, they assured us), and others were local folks. They introduced themselves one by one, some with translators, and spoke humbly but rather confidently of their company experiences. They seemed open to our questions, acting more like giddy school friends talking to outsiders than assembly-line workers. Many of them were earning low wages and doing hard manual labor. They talked of having to build up their physical stamina in order to work there. But they each emphasized how caring Tyson had been toward them and how the company affirmed their individual value. Of course, these were selected workers who have succeeded in the company. But even so, the relaxed smiles of the workers, who had found much dignity in their jobs, surprised us. Something is going on here that is unexpected and even graceful. Before the workers arrived, one of the managers told us that Tyson had for a long time struggled to overcome racial and cultural barriers, but once the rotations began and reforms were implemented, workers from differing ethnic backgrounds began to interact, and some formed very close relationships.

One of the workers, Della, told us she had a special project, a cookbook called *Randall Road Cooking: Sharing and Caring for the Future of the Babies,* the proceeds of which would benefit the March of Dimes. The cookbook contains recipes from the workers at Tyson: Aunt Carrie's potato salad, pollo al vapor, tamale pie . . . and, of course, a recipe for Cornish game hens by the plant manager.

The ivory-billed woodpecker has not been sighted for sixty years. But a group of Cornell ornithologists did spot one in the Cache River in Arkansas recently.[1] Larger than a crow, with distinctive plumage, these handsome woodpeckers "need dead trees for nesting, and logging squeezed out the ivory bill, turning it into an accusatory ghost."[2]

When I was a student at Bucknell University, I studied ornithology as part of a double major in art and animal behavior. I even spent cold January days in a shack by the Susquehanna River taking data for "optimal foraging theory patterns of chickadees." Chickadees keep rather regular hours, coming in each day at similar times to forage, and this pattern could be interpreted with ecological significance. They are efficient, saving their precious energies in a winter riverscape. It is a curious overlap to see the vulnerable birds and their necessary efficiency and the capitalistic efficiencies of our factories today. Both scenes mirror each other, overlapping in the needs of survival. Of course, we would be right to argue that our culture is a culture of wasteful efficiency. We have the capacity to alter and create the environment in ways that seem in some cases ridiculously destructive. In the wanton free-for-all drive to succeed, any capitalistic system craves for more and more. And in that kind of abundance, we are clearly in danger of damaging the delicate ecosystem and of losing our humanity in the process.

Does the spotting of the ivory-billed woodpecker represent part of the humanity we lost? And what did we really see at the kill factory in Springdale, Arkansas? Can we really eat our birds and save them too?

Of course, as we toured Tyson Foods, many of us might have pondered another obvious question related to this: Is it possible to be the CEO of a company and be a Christian? If the answer is yes, you might argue that finding one with much integrity is as difficult as spotting an ivory woodpecker. (By the way, none have been spotted since the last reporting, and ornithologists are bickering over whether the proof of the last sighting is substantiated enough.) As skeptical as our group was when visiting the factory, we had to admit that it took enormous courage for John Tyson to make his faith public by weaving it into the core values of the company.[3] He was very honest with us about the tensions he has to negotiate and the struggles he has gone through as the CEO and as a person. Questions filled our minds. Is it then possible to operate a faith-based company in which some million animals are killed each week? Is Tyson "feeding the country" or simply being consumer driven?

Answers to such questions are never black-and-white. For instance, if these clean, efficient systems did not exist, avian SARS would have destroyed all of us by now. When victims of the tsunami in Indonesia needed food, Tyson filled the order, also with remarkable efficiency. It has the system in place to respond. It is also able to export this system, whereby Cornish hens require only a month or so from hatching to the table. Tyson is providing much needed work to these local soils, creating a little city and culture, along with Wal-Mart, in Bentonville, Arkansas.

And, perhaps most important, if the likes of Tyson Foods did not exist, I am not so sure that, if I were hungry, I could successfully chase and catch a free-range chicken, let alone kill it and prepare it for the table. I would be the first to go extinct, in other words.

Perhaps we are just like the chickadees after all, saving our energies optimally so that we too can survive our winters. We are simply trying to do our best to survive in the competition of the marketplace, finding the most efficient means to eat. But there's a cost to this efficiency. All of the middle managers at Tyson expressed how difficult it was to balance their family and church commitments with the stress of their jobs. These workers are enduring stress so that we can all celebrate Thanksgiving, Christmas, and Easter. These holidays have, ironically, become the high noon of stress and death for many creatures.

Tyson's chaplaincy program, one of the largest in the country, addresses the various needs of the workers, including stress management. But there's an inherent tension and stress in the chaplains' roles as well. The minister we spoke with told of a time when the workers went on a strike. He had to choose whether to march with the union or not. (He did.) After feeling the effects of the intensity of the job, from low-wage workers, to chaplains, to the CEO, I realized that those laser beams of consumerism were not just directed at the birds but at all of us, and we are all being asked, "what is our life about?"

We do long for a day when ivory-billed woodpeckers will roam the dark shadows of Arkansas rivers, eating grubs and worms to their hearts' content. Somehow, though, the ideals of that vision seem dreamlike in the weight of the world's conditions today. In the fiendish and ironic drama of survival and abundance, only the bottom line seems to matter. But what we need to think about is not just the competitive drive of a successful American company but the issue of stewardship of our abundance. It is not the question of to kill or not to kill but of how much sacrifice and for what purpose. The Bible points us to a place of abundance called the Shalom of God. Scripture does not prohibit the killing of animals. But it does deal harshly with our greed, our materialism, and the exploitation of those who are also made in the image of God. Instead, it points to a time when all things will be made beautiful, and every sacrifice is seen as the entry point of beauty. We need the ivory-billed woodpeckers in our lives because we need appreciation of that fleeting vision of the beautiful and of what was lost. Their mysterious dark wings reveal part of what was sacrificed for our material abundance today. Further, the greater challenge may be to see that even a Tyson Cornish hen can point to that sacrificial need in our everyday lives. Can we, with grateful hearts, give thanks to the Giver of life not just for our capacity to survive but for being given a vision of abundant grace?

At the end of our tour of the factory, a youth pastor/writer member of the group commented, "Maybe we should consider sending our kids to observe this kill factory rather than some summer mission trip?" I nodded and reached for my wallet to purchase one of Della's cookbooks. I wanted to participate in the communion of people of dignity, shared through their meals. They are the survivors of the ecosystem of consumerism. And I wanted to know what tamale pie tastes like in Arkansas.

I dream of seeing these woodpeckers someday too. My search for them would be a fabulous way to honor John James Audubon,[4] one of my favorite American artists. These rare creatures are but a ghost of a time past when survival of the fittest was the only reality, back when the harsh ecosystem might have killed more humans in winter than woodpeckers. Now that reality is replaced by convenience and our comfort. Perhaps they were to be spotted only once, but in a fleeting moment. Perhaps they saw us and understood what we have become, and they turned their backs on the world of Wal-Marts and Burger Kings, spreading their wings to fly back into the hot, dark, mysterious swamps of Arkansas, never to be seen again.

August 2005

Photo by Makoto Fujimura, Water Flames Exhibit, 2004, New York City.

XVIII

Planting Seedlings in Stone: Art in New York City

Art is both agrarian and urban. It is both the farm and the city. Every artist is integrating, or should be attempting to integrate, earthy, bodily humanity with communal urban constructs: the blending of Nature with City. As I work in my studio in New York City, the agrarian vision for simplicity and the harmonized stewardship of nature are disclosed as I stretch Japanese handmade paper for the surface of my paintings. The result of more than a millennium of Japanese stewardship is reflected in the layers of fiber of the Cloud Skin paper that I use. But at the same time, as I layer gold leaf on the paper, it creates an urban, Mondrian-like grid, like windows into the divine soul. The grid is a symbol of the City of God descending into our cities.

In Chelsea, now the mecca of the contemporary art scene, I had a major New York exhibit called *Water Flames* in 2004. All of my art seeks the soul, using medieval Japanese materials while taking inspiration from T. S. Eliot and Dante. After 9/11 I began to seek a language of reconciliation via art and poetry, a journey that took me to Eliot's *Four Quartets*, his last masterpiece from the 1940s, and, via Eliot, Dante's *The Divine Comedy*, written in the 1300s. Both Eliot and Dante journey upward from the "Waste Land" to the "still point," from "dark lost woods" to "Empyrean," the highest of heavens. As I sought to recover the spiritual, and exilic, language of hope, Water Flames became a visual depiction of the City of God, using the language of abstraction that was developed by modern masters such as Arschile Gorky[1] and Mark Rothko.[2] Both artists integrated, sometimes literally, the sublime, organic shapes of nature with the urban interiors of New York City. Their compelling vision for a dying world of lost souls, via abstraction, grappled honestly with an invisible reality. In my art I consciously link the works of abstract expressionists and sixteenth-century Japanese artists, such as Tohaku Hasegawa's *Shorinzu Byobu*, a profound painting of pine forests that depicts the "sound of silence."

In every museum, actually, this City-Nature integration is carried out. If you are fortunate enough to go to the Metropolitan Museum this winter, where there are currently two "once-in-a-lifetime" exhibits, the paintings of Fra Angelico and the drawings of Vincent van Gogh, you can witness these masters' careful steward-ship of their craft. This exhibit traces an extraordinary melding of the birth of urbanity (the Renaissance) and the translation of agrarian visual landscape into a complex set of calligraphic swirls and twirls (mostly drawn in the last three years of van Gogh's life). Fra Angelico looked for the heavenly city in Florence, a place where medieval trees and plants filled the streets and where her inhabitants danced toward paradise. Van Gogh, exiled from both the church and the cities, tried to invent an echo of that paradise—in agrarian scenes, in cypress trees, in farmers sowing seeds, in stars that heralded hope and faith—for a vision of restoration.

However, it's not just at the Met that this vision can be seen. This kind of integra-tion can be discovered in concert halls, at dance recitals, in the details of architec-ture, and in every art form.

At the same time, disintegration is also unfolding. In the corrupted human condi-tion that hijacks the process of creativity, that blindly forges a new world of engross-ment, we disrupt the process of integration. The main cause of this corruption, or the pollution in the aesthetic river of culture, is self-aggrandizement and a type of embezzlement made in the name of advancing the creative arts. As a culture, we do not know how best to address and speak about this problem. We think that any type of progress is good; for instance, in the fifties the Anaconda factory in

Hastings-on-Hudson dumped gallons and gallons of chemicals into the beautiful Hudson, calling the blackened river a sign of progress. We pollute the cultural landscape with irresponsible expressions in the name of progress and call them freedom of speech. Thus, our cultural landscape is increasingly uninhabitable. If we cannot dwell inside the imaginative landscape of what is offered, then what is the purpose of creativity?

The Suburb of Hell

One symptom of the cultural disconnection between the art produced in cities and the cultural realities of regional America is evident in the media. The media feeds upon the fragmentation and fear between the urban and the agrarian. Journalism today seems content to operate only in sensationalism, echoing the same systemic ills of the art world. This disconnect affects us all, contributing to a greater cultural disengagement and to distrust and cynicism. But the fine arts do serve as upstream sources of cultural expression, for good or for ill. Therefore, we need to begin to address the source — if we are to effect positive change.

I think Suzi Gablik,[3] a maverick critic and art historian, was correct when she redefined the art world as "the suburb of hell."[4] Not the inferno itself, but a suburb of it. A suburb erects secure fences around its inhabitants in order to make sure that comforts and security are not violated. The rules are clear there. Thus, the white boxes of clean Chelsea galleries are shielded in their elitism from the outside world. Underneath the guise of authentic expression and the wild expressions of art are layers of implicit rules, and a twisted accord — or at least a détente — with her systemic ills. Artists end up competing against each other like contestants in a *Survivor* episode. The result is that their desire to fight and to expose the greed and darkness in large canvases ends up subdivided into manageable but explosive bits: "small shocks" bought and sold like any other cheap trinket on Canal Street. Their idealistic ambitions to voice antiauthority and anticorporate visions often become mired in their own greed and corruption. They crave authenticity but end up stealing ideas from the vulnerable and the innocent, even to the detriment of friends and peers. And we can, and many do, justify such action in the name of freedom of expression. Artists hope to escape accountability, to be their own masters, but end up being enslaved by expensive addictions. Artists want the world to change but end up in a narcissistic shell of their own creation. Those who play the game skillfully will end up with millions of dollars for creating expressions for shock, that will be a background for the rich and the powerful, who love to own their personal "biting the hands that feed you" kind of imagery.

But on 9/11 we woke up to a nightmare in that suburbia. What artists considered shocking in the 1990s (remember the Sensation exhibit of young British artists at the Brooklyn Museum in 1999) was mere child's play within whitewashed walls of pretense. The real hell that opened itself up was only a mile away and was all too real. Like some grotesque gaping mouth of a Hieronymus Bosch painting, Ground Zero swallowed up the superficialities of her surroundings. The real fire was full of fury, impossible to tame or contain.

So, today, we are reexamining the art of our times. What will the future tell people about our time? Will the most sensationalistic art of the late twentieth century, such as Jeff Koons' media-savvy pop objects and Matthew Barney's inveterate blurring of Genesis boundaries, seem merely facile in a world of international terrorism and Columbine mass murder? Will Fra Angelico's and van Gogh's works speak more boldly into the twenty-first century than in the twentieth century? *The Shock of the New*, the title of a seminal book Robert Hughes wrote in the 1980s about twentieth-century art, seems less than shocking or hardly new in a fear-filled world of DNA manipulation and nuclear terrorism. And why is it that we seem determined to persist in the wanton debasement of ourselves, creating imaginative hells in our post-human times? Are there any signs of hope? Of recovery?

Carrying the Dust of Eden

In *Rivers and Tides*, a remarkable 2001 documentary, Scottish artist Andy Goldsworthy recounts his experience as an art school student. He describes how he discovered that for him the studio was the beach on the way to the school, the ocean, and, consequently, the world. By moving out of the confines of a typical classroom studio, he found that the world became the greater studio, where his environmental and documentary works can thrive. Goldsworthy's works symbolize how the fine arts can have a direct impact as an agent transforming the world.

Goldsworthy's journey from his studio outward is a parable of the contemporary call to recover the arts' role in mediating between Nature and City. City artists must reconnect with farmers—with their home regions and their agrarian vision. Like Goldsworthy, we must recover the language of nature, of the ephemeral, of the rhythm of shepherds and the cotton fields, of the river rock and boulders of tidal rivers teeming with salmon. But I also contend that this careful negotiation requires a more direct look at the cities of ashes, the void that exists in the ground zeroes of the world, because the hell of the artistic imagination, one might argue, is the only real point of departure to create today.

Theologically speaking, we are all living in the ashes of Ground Zero, in our own Waste Land. But we carry the dust of Eden in our DNA. Now, as we face a world of Katrinas and earthquakes, of atomic devastation and bullet holes in public schools, we need to understand that our imaginative capacities carry a responsibility to heal, every bit as much as they carry a responsibility to depict angst. Instead of exerting the artistic imagination to destructive, exploitive ends, we need, as van Gogh did in his drawings, to sow the seeds of renewal and hope. Ours is the exilic land of Babylon, where Jeremiah exhorted the people of God to "seek the peace and prosperity of the city" (Jeremiah 29:7). Often, cities are where "craftsmen and the artisans" are taken into captivity (see Jeremiah 29:2). If we are to see art as an integrative force, then we must recover the language of hope in exile. Then art can lead in the reconciliation between City and Nature. This view borrows heavily from the vision of a New Jerusalem. The true City of God is a city full of shalom trees; it's a city through which runs a shining river of life, the true fulfillment of our creative ambitions.

At a National Council on the Arts meeting, former council member and philanthropist Philip Hanes exhorted us to be diligent in our work, since, as he insisted, "the information age, for us, is over. China and India are well ahead of us already; we have entered the creative age." If Hanes and Thomas Friedman (*The World Is Flat*) are correct, and the only thing that cannot be outsourced is creativity, then isn't this good news for artists?

A Vision for Dignity

The creative age will require, though, integration or the reconciliation of the heart of the city with the (rural) country's open air and spaces. That means children living in the dilapidated ghettos of cities — the majority being immigrant children — need the strategy of engagement with the New World. Rafe Esquith, a teacher at Hobart Elementary School in Los Angeles, demonstrated with his Shakespeare program for children who do not yet speak English that it is possible for immigrant children to give prominence to the voices of civilization. Mayors (and now state governors) can look to Mayor Joseph Riley of Charleston as an inspiration for helping to start the Mayors' Institute on City Design with the National Endowment for the Arts. In a National Council for the Arts meeting, Mayor Riley humbly stated, "We mayors exhaust ourselves with lots of decisions — political, personnel, and budget. But one hundred years from now, there will be no real evidence of how we made those decisions. In contrast, a decision about the physical design of a city will influence the city and its people for generations." Now we are able to rely on a twenty-year knowledge base to assist in the wake of Katrina. Council members just approved a grant to go toward a collaborative venture with Habitat for Humanity and the Mayors' Institute to rebuild not only houses but beautiful, well-designed homes. In such restoration we need to provide not just temporary shelters but a vision for dignity via the beauty of the buildings and cities we build.

The new Governors' Institute on Community Design, which takes this significant design dialogue to the state level, is cosponsored by the U.S. Government's National Endowment for the Arts and its Environmental Protection Agency. Strange bedfellows? No, it's smart to connect the two — again, it's an issue of stewardship. The best design is most efficient and friendly to the environment. The best design considers what the community needs first, even the needs of her voiceless inhabitants. The best design brings beauty into our lives. If only I could see the same design dialogue around the rebuilding of the Freedom Tower, which will be built two blocks from my home. I am disappointed that Libeskind's transcendental original design has now been turned, via the dysfunctional meddling of many, into a Fortress Tower.

Agrarians see the city as the epitome of dysfunction: a dystopic vision of ideals gone awry. But when in their path of individualized self-reliance, writers and artists write in opposition to the city, they are also contributing to this unnecessary divide. Do they not also, along with city artists, need the infrastructure of the city's publishing worlds to communicate to a larger audience? The agrarian roots of Millet and van Gogh and the expansive vision of the Hudson School Painters flow right through the heart of a city. Perhaps it is the recovery of these roots that will feed back into the renewal of culture.

As I jog the promenade of Hudson River Park, I am reminded of these things. I see the empty Ground Zero, which now beckons our imaginative engagement and healing. I see the Hudson, now closer to the beauty it once was, thanks to a few courageous fishermen and a custodian at Anaconda factory named Fred Danback (see Bill Moyers' PBS special *America's First River: Moyers on the Hudson*), who fought the company in the 1960s with a groundbreaking suit and won, thereby ushering in decades of environmental recovery. Now, with so many families inhabiting lower Manhattan, largely because of a cleaner New York City, I can see the promise of the New World, with the Statue of Liberty and Ellis Island, still being fulfilled here. And as I pass the Jewish Heritage (Holocaust) Museum, where I can see Andy Goldsworthy's installation of oak trees planted in crevices of rocks, I pray. We need the creative, the faithful, who would together incarnate their creative gifts in the hearts of urban reality, in today's ground zeroes. We need those centered souls to find their identities in collaboration. We need, in short, a movement: not a movement of multiphrenic activities but a movement of stillness. New York City needs to become a "still point of the turning world." We need more creative visionaries who would dare even to plant seedlings in stone that will mature into trees whose roots will crack open the rock, as if it were a mere egg, spilling its *shalom* dirt into the heart of a city.[5]

August 2005

Ty Fujimura, touring Syracuse University.

XIX

Walking Backward into the Future

We have been taking our eldest son, Ty, on college tours, traveling mostly up and down the East Coast. Having been raised in New York City, he's been curiously interested in only city schools. He's described some of the schools he has visited as "an enclave of pseudo-community." Perhaps so, but I've been reminding him that some of the best education can be had in such enclaves (such as Bucknell University, where my wife and I went). Perhaps being able to focus in a quiet bubble does have some merit, I suggested. So far, my son is not buying it.

The climate of college selection has changed much since I went through it in the seventies. When my son and I were visiting Cornell University, where I also took a tour with my father, I realized how much things have evolved since then. Colleges are big businesses and self-assured marketing machines. Their successes are made visible in so many new building constructions. New York University and Columbia are buying up New York City, and practically every college we visited is expanding. But, as my son and I migrate from the Hampton Inns, filled with seniors and their parents, all with the same looks of inevitability, to well-marked admission buildings, we have discovered a new art form: Student tour guides are now trained to walk backward and to project their voices at the same time.

Not so when I toured colleges as a teenager way back when. We meekly followed the guides around the campus, walking the grounds without looking for any amenities. When did a college education begin to involve new sports complexes with Crunch-like, fully equipped weight and exercise rooms, accompanying trainers, and rock-climbing walls? Back then, we toured the libraries and soaked it all in seriously, but somewhat casually. College tours today have evolved into individual performances worthy of rating and timing, much like a skating competition. I suppose in the competitive business of education, with so much at stake, it pays to train students to walk backward in order to save time. Perhaps it speaks of the confidence that colleges place in their own students, to equip them with such indispensable training for life. Aside from the technical requirements of such a performance—such as projecting their voices, not tripping on the cracks in the sidewalks, getting prospective students and their parents back in time for their "informational meeting" to answer how we can possibly afford this education, or not getting run over by a car (although they assured us that cars in the campus always stop for pedestrians)—there's the human, artistic element that needs to be cultivated for an excellent college tour guide. Humor, the ability to pull out questions from prospective students, and the handling of anxious parents to make them feel at ease all combine to make college tours (if you are privileged to take one from a good guide) a rather intriguing affair.

Over time, my son and I have become experts at rating the tours. If the guide gives cookies in the middle of the tour in one of the college's many neon-lit cafeterias, our rating goes up. If the tour guide is too nervous, we try to bear with that. But the worst tours are usually not the student's fault but are weather-related (a blizzard in Syracuse—minus ten points!) or are colleges too calculated with excessive marketing (for instance, a video piece showing many athletes and the diverse student body, all smiling in their successes—a huge deduction in Ty's mind).

So as we toured campuses, I naturally began to ponder not just what makes a good tour guide but what makes a good education in general. After discussing this topic at one school's Asian cafeteria in Baltimore (yes, having good sushi in the cafeteria earns a few points), we decided that a good education is learning to walk backward into the future. Perhaps these college tour guides do have something to teach us after all.

My wife and I raised our three children to, indeed, walk backward, to respect the tradition and history from which they have come. Rather than promising them an unlimited future, I found myself teaching my children to steward carefully the gifts they have. I want them to know the best of artistic heritages, from Shakespeare and Bach to Hemingway. Also I want them to know how much their own time echoes in the various chambers of history and is relevant in their post-9/11 experience. I want them to understand that as a product of Judy's (Irish/English/Scottish) and my (Japanese and God knows what else[1]) mixed-race-and-culture marriage, they represent in their mixed blood the very promise of reconciliation of two nations that once were at war. However, I do not want our children to dwell there but to walk confidently toward a goal on their own path. We have tried to teach them that success is not the worldly attainment of money and fame but that success is being faithful to the unique journey God has called them to. Education must be past-focused and future-focused at the same time. Our job as parents is to help our children discover the uniqueness of their calling that only they can walk in.

Paul Elie, in *The Life You Save May Be Your Own: An American Pilgrimage*, poignantly looked back to portray the journeys of Flannery O'Connor, Doris Day, Walker Percy, and Thomas Merton. As he recounted the life and art of Flannery O'Connor, arguably the most influential writer of the mid-twentieth century, he noted that at age five, O'Connor trained one of her chickens to walk backward. A reporter from New York City somehow found this out at the time and took a newsreel, with the title *Unique Chicken Goes in Reverse*:

> The episode lasts less than a minute. Yet Mary Flannery
> O'Connor had been changed by it. She perceived that she had
> an unusual gift, even if it was just a gift for getting a certain
> kind of chicken to walk a certain way; and she saw that her
> challenge in life would be to make the nature of her gift clear to
> people who wouldn't understand it otherwise. . . . The chicken
> was a freak, a grotesque, and when a cameraman came all the
> way from New York to Savannah to photograph her just because
> she had trained it, she was suddenly a kind of freak, too.[2]

O'Connor's early experience shaped the vocabulary of her fiction. It seems that she not only trained her chicken to walk backward, but she also trained herself to write and see in a kind of backward manner. She reversed the conventionalities of a southern worldview with a wry critical stance, exposing the superficial evils of a "Christ-haunted south." Her characters, such as The Misfit in "A Good Man Is Hard to Find" or Hazel Motes in *Wise Blood*, speak out of the violent cores of our existence, so explosive and obsessive yet devastatingly precise in their actions. They will not be comfortably shaped into the future, but they resolutely and awkwardly remain in their pasts, walking reverse in a kind of self-tormenting labyrinth.

But by inviting us to walk in that labyrinth, O'Connor gently lighted the grace journey that lies deep beneath our feet. She walked backward into a unique world, projecting her voice in an anguished, compressed scream, but what she actually described was a transformative, rather hopeful, series of epiphanies, intentionally cast into our own evil-filled darkness and desires. What she accomplished in her short stories and two novels (she died very young) is noteworthy, exactly because these stories arise from an unexpected place of exile, the voice of a Catholic in the Protestant South. Her stories look backward, influenced by Dante and Shakespeare but also mapping a new territory of contemporary fiction. O'Connor's stories seem fantastic and freakish at first, but we do grow into them, as we are so much in need of their vigor today, her dark vision so filled with faith.

As I negotiated the I-95 to get Ty and me home, and as he recited *Hamlet* for his senior literature class, I pondered how much of our education is about the past and how much is about the future. Of course, it is about both. I then realized that Ty has been walking backward already, without much fanfare. Whenever students decide to stay true to their faith as a Christian in a public school in New York City, as Ty has, they are walking backward. Whenever young people are committed to keeping themselves sexually pure, as Ty has endeavored to do with his girlfriend, they are walking backward into the currents of cultural norms. When they, like Ty (with a Jewish buddy), decide on their own to start a conservative club in their liberal Quaker school, they are definitely walking backward. Ty's teachers and fellow students may not agree with him, but he manages with humor. No matter where he ends up or what he chooses to do in the future, my son knows what it means to negotiate the labyrinth of complex pluralism of our day. The key, I realized for him, as well as for me, is walking backward and at the same time paying attention to what comes ahead. That takes a kind of zany, awkward commitment not normally encouraged in schools nor in the world. More important, such a stance forces him to lead others, projecting his voice and assuring them that their decision matters too.

So, we anxiously await his decision on his future, wondering how we ourselves ever got accepted by any college. I have learned much from these tour guides. Art today too suffers from certain amnesia. ("Post-modernism is xenophobic to the past,"[3] stated Tom Oden, a noted theologian.) Perhaps the best of art too is made via a backward glance rather than simply blindly forging ahead, or we may end up, like O'Connor's characters, trapped in futility. Perhaps by paying careful attention to the historical landmarks around us and by artfully describing the milieu via naming new experiences, we will stumble onto a vision that maps a new territory for art. Whether or not we buy into the hype of college admissions, one thing is for sure: The twenty-first century will be led by creative children who boldly dare to lead backward. Their voices, like Flannery O'Connor's, will project into future corridors of their making, and we shall indeed be glad for that. To have such guides is worth any price, any sacrifice.

November 2005

PS Our Cornell guide did receive the highest points of all the guides so far.
PPS Ty is now attending New York University, majoring in math.

XX

The Housewife That Could

"Designing a dream city is easy," Jane Jacobs concluded. "Rebuilding a living one takes imagination."[1]

Jane Jacobs passed away a few days ago at the age of eighty-nine in a Toronto hospital. A day later several flowers were placed in front of 555 Hudson Street in Greenwich Village, New York City, with a note that said, "From this house, in 1961, a housewife changed the world."

Last February after a worship service at my church, I had lunch across from 555 Hudson Street with sociologist Tony Carnes. We were in a Chinese restaurant, looking across to the White Horse Tavern on Hudson Street. "You know Jane Jacobs lived here, right?" he asked me. If there's anything I have learned in New York City, it is that you want to listen to an urban sociologist.

What is so significant about Jane Jacobs? Well, according to Tony, and many others, she is the mother of a movement called New Urbanism, and, yes, she happened to save Greenwich Village and change the world, standing up against the behemoth of highway construction and also against one of the most powerful men to control the destiny of New York, Robert Moses. Moses, who began his illustrious career by designing the New York World's Fair of 1939, is attributed with single-handedly creating the suburbia of Long Island (and the development of suburbia in general) and the birth of car culture. He was so successful that no one stood against him in power and influence.

In 1961, Robert Moses met his match. During a hearing at which he announced his plans to open a highway into Washington Square, through Greenwich Village, Jane Jacobs and several housewives stormed the hearing. Moses was irate, saying, "There is nobody against this—NOBODY, NOBODY, NOBODY, but a bunch of, a bunch of MOTHERS!"[2]

Today, many attribute Jane Jacobs with having defeated Moses in this modern version of David and Goliath. New Urbanist James Howard Kunstler wrote:

> One can say pretty definitively that she won the battle and the war, though the enormous inertia of American culture still acts as a drag on a genuine civic revival here. By the mid 1960s, her interests and writings broadened to take in the wider issues of economics and social relations, and by force of intellect she compelled the cultural elite to take seriously this untrained female generalist—and wonderful prose stylist—who had the nerve to work out large ideas on her own. Naturally, her books are now part of the [New Urbanist] curriculum.[3]

As she and her housewife friends battled Robert Moses, Jane Jacobs wrote a book called *The Death and Life of Great American Cities*. It became a foundational text for those who challenged the conventional notion of urban growth and progress. She argued for diversity of close-knit streets and buildings and for dense populations that would increase commerce and community, an urban concoction that even provides safety. Suburbia, a legacy of Moses, would by contrast pretend to provide safety and protection, but, according to Jacobs, it would ultimately isolate and dehumanize. She was often asked if her ideas came about from hanging out with intellectuals at the White Horse Tavern. No, she would answer, I could not afford to go there. She merely could observe from her window, with her curious eyes roaming the streets of Greenwich Village, the intricacies of street life both ugly and beautiful. What she saw there was not a scene of destruction, filled with gangs and prostitutes. What she saw was a city teeming with dialogue, neighborly attention, and a fermenting, vibrant cultural mix that would fight the dehumanizing elements of our increasingly segmented modern culture. More important, as she raised her children, she imagined a better city.

One might wonder, *Safety? How could the chaos and brokenness of city life provide safety?* If Jane Jacobs were alive today, her answer might be something like this: It would be difficult for a Columbine-type incident to break out in one of New York's schools today, however dangerous and tenuous it might be. City life limits crime simply because there are more eyes to keep watch. Besides, it would be very, very difficult for teenage boys to hide a cache of automatic weapons in a one-hundred-square-foot bedroom. Urbanity forces us to be dependent on each other and to deal with our neighbors. Urbanity forces us out of our comfort zones and may even expose our dark, sinister plans.

Should we not pause in order to listen to a housewife named Jane Jacobs? Today, as we max out our credit cards, purchasing gasoline in our four-dollar-a-gallon culture, should we not question Robert Moses' insistent vision for progress and the expansion of highways?

As I volunteer on the National Council on the Arts and get to know the NEA design director, Jeff Speck,[4] who is overseeing the Mayor's Institute as an urban design expert, I am constantly reminded of the power of design to directly affect our quality of life. In this arena of New Urbanism, the arts do overlap with our lives. Our cities are our artwork, and their designs can make us either more human or less human. Whether one agrees with the pro-growth model of Moses or the organic vision of Jacobs, this imaginative battle of how we are to see our cities continues today.

As I walked with my soon-to-be teenage daughter on Bleecker Street in Greenwich Village recently, I had to give a nod to Jane Jacobs' instincts. Bleecker Street is the most sought-after cultural nexus and originator of new commerce, far more influential, in my view, than the hyper-commerce sites, such as The Shops at Columbus Circle. Why else would fashion designers such as Marc Jacobs seek out tiny spaces on Bleecker Street? Why else would *Saturday Night Live* comedians celebrate Magnolia Bakery, also on Bleecker Street, with their ode to *The Chronicles of Narnia*? Why else would Japanese magazines feature Bleecker Street stores to the extent that if you were to walk Bleecker in early May, Japan's Golden Week, it would be filled with so many Japanese that you would think you were in Shibuya, Tokyo? Where else would my creative second son C. J. go to get his left-handed acoustic guitar? (To Matt Umanov Guitars on Bleecker, of course, because "they have guitars that really sing.") And where else could you run into a friendly pastor of a storefront church, appropriately named the Neighborhood Church (it's next to Matt Umanov's)? And, most important for that beautiful spring day, where would you find birthday gifts that could not be bought anywhere else for the soon-to-be twelve-year-old friend of your daughter? Bleecker Street.

Jane Jacobs was right. A city is best when its buildings are diverse and small, where we can enjoy diversity of class, backgrounds, and ages mingling together in compressed streets. Today, such an environment is so needed, so endangered. The city is fast becoming a destination site for tourism, as well as a place of commerce and a family-friendly shopping center, despite the high rent. Whether one agrees with Jacobs' many irascible perspectives (and she was prolific in that, as well), one must admit that she did forge a context for how a creative city can be imagined. Whatever is done today around America in favor of creative neighborhoods, we all owe a nod of thanks to Jacobs.

It is noted that when Jane Jacobs did her dishes or walked about the local streets, people would hear her audibly debate with Thomas Jefferson and, as a second alternative, Ben Franklin. This exercise was not a joke to her but a serious interplay among generalists of equal statures across the schism of centuries, navigating the complex pluralism of our time. Similarly, anyone today walking about New York City or any other urban mazes of the day would need to, and want to, hold debates (and perhaps wash dishes too) with Jane Jacobs, a determined housewife imagining a better city with her Remington typewriter. The sound of her typing echoes in our neighborly streets, refracting the dense, fiery heart of our humanity.

Jane Jacobs won the battle to save Greenwich Village. I am glad she did.

May 2006

Madonna and Child, Fra Angelico. Alinari/Art Resource, NY.
Galleria Sabauda, Turin, Italy

XXI

Fra Angelico and the Five-Hundred-Year Question

It all started when I visited the Fra Angelico (1395–1455) exhibit at the Met last December. Behind the splendor of the Christmas crèche, I entered the back hall of the museum. Surprisingly, the exhibit had no line (as opposed to the van Gogh drawing exhibit, which had a wait of forty-five minutes). But a hushed gathering was moving about in the darkly lit halls.

I entered the halls, and the golden aura of a diminutive Virgin Mary painting greeted me, with her azurite robe and the Christ child's supple body reflecting her humanity — a simple work full of weighty colors. After a few seconds of pondering the saturated surface, I had to close my eyes. I realized this was too much to behold all at once. As I staggered about looking for a blank wall to stare at, almost feeling ashamed to be in the presence of such greatness, the "five-hundred-year" question popped into my mind.

What is the five-hundred-year question? Well, it's a long-term, historical look at the reality of our cultures that asks, What ideas, what art, what vision in our current culture has the capacity to affect humanity for more than five hundred years? It's the opposite of the Warholian "fifteen minutes of fame." It's also a question I raise to my teenagers, whose culture celebrates immediate gratification, also seeking after "fifteen minutes of fame." If our decisions matter and make ripple effects in the world, then should we not weigh what we say and do in light of the five-hundred-year question?

Contemporary art does not encourage such thoughts. Except for a few notable exceptions, like video guru Bill Viola or the minimal zen of painter Agnes Martin, contemporary artists want to compress, rather than stretch, time. Both Viola's meditative video installations and the simple striped paintings of Martin force us to slow down to experience the art and to consider the historical link beyond modernism. We are immersed in a visual culture that squeezes life into fifteen-second commercials with instant gains. Chelsea galleries are full of art that screams for attention, as if they are the twenty-first-century version of Willy Loman, the disillusioned salesman in *Death of a Salesman*. "Attention, attention must be paid to such an art," call out gallerists dressed in their designer fashions. Rather than profundity, they pine after instant recognition and fame. Just like Willy, we peddle our goods to find significance and survival, all the more as the gray world around us passes by.

[margin note: or deep knowledge of meaning]

Meanwhile, artists who labor to develop their craft, artists who are committed to a longer view of their art, suffer. I can name many midcareer artists in their fifties who deserve much attention, but galleries ignore them and give fresh-out-of-art-school artists solo exhibits. Of course, they are replaced the following year by the next round of twenty-year-olds.

Nothing wrong with twenty-year-olds, by the way: Fra Angelico was one, but that's the year he entered the Dominican order, where his gift was discovered in the long-lasting tradition of art. He was trained as an apprentice, and his first notable piece was a visual echo of Lorenzo Monaco, which suggests that he studied under the Italian gothic master.

If Fra Angelico were alive today, he would have a hard time being apprenticed or finding anyone to teach him his craft, let alone joining an order. The church is not the first place a creative genius would look to be trained in art. That statement alone reveals how much Christians have abdicated our responsibility to steward culture. *[margin note: Failed at]*

If you spoke with those people staggering about in the Met with me, having a similar reaction to looking at the glory of Fra Angelico's paintings, you may find them to be enlightened secularists who also grieve over the fragmentation, the loss of a spiritual anchor in the contemporary art scene. They may even be atheists who by the very essence of their denial have to appreciate the sheer weighty anchor of Fra Angelico's paintings. Atheism demands a language of belief to wrestle against. Fra Angelico's paintings are undeniably Christian to the core. Enlightened secularists would be staggering because the Spirit has left them. Atheists would stagger because they have lost the defining opposition. As a Christian, I stagger and grieve because I do not see anyone on the horizon who creates and paints today who would rival Fra Angelico's angelic weight.

In short, we are all staggering about, or should be . . . those who have eyes to see. That is precisely how we should react to Fra Angelico and the five-hundred-year question. We stagger because we have lost even our ability to ask that question.

So I took the subway home and Googled "the 1500s." During that century the Tudors ruled the early Renaissance, having ended the Wars of the Roses in 1485. In 1503, da Vinci painted the *Mona Lisa*, and Michelangelo created *David*. Not a bad start. The Sistine Chapel and *The Last Supper*, of course, would follow. Christopher Columbus was sailing to sites unknown, trying again to get to Asia. Magellan noted the global shape of the earth. Martin Luther posted his ninety-five theses on the Wittenberg door (1517). And very significant for me, Hasegawa Tohaku, the Michelangelo of Japan, was born (1539).

I closed my eyes again, and the angels of Fra Angelico reinvited themselves in.

Will we see another Renaissance in the days to come? Will we have another chance to steward our culture, without losing our identity and faith in the process?

You might be saying, "How can we think about five hundred years from now if we have the capacity to blow ourselves up a thousand times over? Aren't you being a bit optimistic?"

Recently, I had a conversation with a Japanese art student who asked me, "How can you paint if you know that you may not be around ten years from now?" The look on her face told me that she was deadly serious. Even after all these years,

Japanese youth grow up, apparently, with the shadow of Hiroshima and Nagasaki. So I guided her to the ages that led up to the 1500s, and I shared with her about the period of world history in which Fra Angelico painted.

It was not a cozy time in history. The stenches of Black Death hovered all over Europe and Asia. Remember, the plague killed half, yes half, of the population in Europe. The swords of assassination were drawn (striking the Dukes of Surrey and Exeter, and then the Earls of Kent, Huntington, and Salisbury for Richard II), and the church was in turmoil (two popes resigned and one was excommunicated in the span of four years). The Ottoman Empire invaded Constantinople, ending the Byzantine Age. No, it was not an age to have hope or to think in terms of the next five hundred years. In fact, the list of events seems to have remarkable similarities to our times.[1]

So how did Fra Angelico manage to paint these indelible images? Perhaps the more pertinent question is, To what hope did he cling in such a dark time?

After my third visit to the Fra Angelico exhibit, I allowed myself to drink deeply of that hope. It is the hope not only of an individual genius but also of patronage, of society, and of the church. I realized that in order to create today—in fact, in order to live today—I desperately need Fra Angelico in my imagination. Then the angelic faces would fill my heart as I pondered Thomas Aquinas; I would consider the life of Saint Francis (who appears over and over in the Met exhibit), the saint and artist of two centuries past who ushered in the resplendence of the Renaissance via his humanity, injecting creativity and theater back into theology.[2] I wondered if, had I painted with Fra Angelico, I would hear about the dangerous teenage heretic in France named Joan of Arc (executed in 1431). Perhaps then I would turn to the last panel of my own *The Last Judgment* and paint Joan of Arc's face (secretly, of course) as she danced up the stairs of heaven in her rich cinnabar robe with golden calligraphy, a design fit for a queen.[3]

In such a cultural environment, an artist does not need to be consciously thinking in five-hundred-year terms: He or she will be cultivated by the norms of society and encouraged to seek beyond the immediate, to do all things unto God. In other words, if we are truly cognizant of the only audience that would count—God—we are already asking the five-hundred-year question.

I've heard many Christians say, "Why should we care about art and culture when we know that all will be burned up in the coming judgment? Aren't our souls the only thing that is eternal? Should we not be focused on saving souls?"[4] Yes, absolutely, we should be concerned about our souls, but to what end are we saved? The Bible, from Genesis to Revelation, notes the Creator God infusing his goodness into the creation and then using his children to fulfill creation's purposes. Those who are called to be children of God (see Romans 8) are to exercise their creative gift to become vessels of God's Holy Spirit, to partake in the creation of the New Order. While God does have the power to destroy all that is wicked and sinful, he often chooses to sanctify (as in gold) rather than burn away (as in dross), transforming our works. As the Bible makes it clear that God's desire is that the children of God be sanctified, surprisingly, God also will sanctify our works, so that our works may last beyond Christ's Judgment Day (see 1 Corinthians 3). The Bible is filled with this promise of an enduring culture of God.[5] If we are saved for both the new heaven *and* the new earth, then we had better begin "storing up treasures" by bringing eternal grace into our ordinary, earthly days. This is what Fra Angelico's works attest to, and when we enter into his world, we, too, are filled with hope of things to come.

Can such eternity refract through our earthly visions? Can my children's world birth generations of geniuses, as did Fra Angelico's heirs, whose splendors would fill the earth as well as heaven? That is the five-hundred-year question, and the answer to that question could grant us the cultural vision for our new century.

June 2006

Plate A

Plate B

XXII

Come and See: Leonardo da Vinci's Philip in The Last Supper

"Nazareth! Can anything good come from there?" Nathanael asked.
"Come and see," said Philip.

John 1:46

The glass door automatically shut behind us as the guide motioned us to enter the inner chamber. We waited, and as another door opened, the cool, dry air enveloped us—a contrast to the July heat in Milan. The courtyard of Santa Maria delle Grazie sparkled in the morning sun, and I wondered if Leonardo da Vinci stood upon the same rocks that I saw here, five hundred years ago.

I had received several inquiries to see if I would comment on *The Da Vinci Code*, and my mind kept wandering back to the same problem: I have never seen Leonardo's *The Last Supper* in person. How could I comment on something that I have not seen? Yes, I own a magnified version of the photograph of the painting (see on adjacent page), represented in a magnificent book by the University of Chicago (440 pages of delight). And I have pondered the image as I have thought much about Andy Warhol's series by the same title. Yes, I had seen a *reproduction* of Leonardo's *The Last Supper*. But I had never stood under the original. So I came to Milan, Italy, to stand under a painting.

"If you want to 'understand' something," said my friend Bruce Herman, "you have to be willing to 'stand under' it." Bruce, an art professor, went on to cite C. S. Lewis's book *An Experiment in Criticism*, in which Lewis, a medieval literature scholar at Oxford University, wrote the following:

> We sit down before the picture in order to have something done
> to us, not that we may do things with it. The first demand any
> work of art makes upon us is surrender. Look. Listen. Receive.
> Get yourself out of the way.[1]

Lewis made a distinction between "using" art and "receiving" art. He argued quite persuasively that "'using' is inferior to 'reception' because art, if used rather than received, merely facilitates, brightens, relieves or palliates our life, and does not add to it."

Why is it important to experience a work firsthand?

If we base our conclusions on what an "expert" has said, or on our own limited assumptions about the work, it remains merely hearsay. We never get to discover, and ultimately exercise, our own creativity out of an authentic experience.

Here's what I discovered standing under *The Last Supper*: The most important visual catalyst for the painting is not the effeminate John or Judas or even Jesus himself. The key figure in kick-starting the visual movement of the painting is Philip.

Philip's outstretched, distressed body and his cinnabar robe are what we see first in the painting's visual theater. The whole painting is first experienced via Philip's body. Our eyes go first to him; afterward they traverse to Jesus, the center of the work. Jesus' mouth is slightly opened (discovered through recent restoration efforts) and his hands are making powerfully emotive gestures. Leonardo was capturing the moment of Jesus' announcement, "I tell you the truth, one of you is going to betray me" (John 13:21).

Leonardo painted for a small space in a grand, dominating scale. Even from the far back of the refectory, it is difficult for the eye to decipher the whole painting all at once. Leonardo painted *The Last Supper* in such a way as to force the viewer to enter the painting, physically and emotionally, and to viscerally become part of the narrative.

Only when standing under the painting can it be seen for what was intended (see plate A, *The Last Supper* painting). Leonardo had a specific visual message for those who stand under the painting. He had the visual sophistication to carry off what very few artists could even dream to do, then and now: He painted the complex psychology of betrayal. It starts with Philip and ends in a moneybag. Invited to walk into Leonardo's funhouse of mirrors, we are all meant to be part of this narrative, forever refracting within our own dark journeys.

As an artist, I naturally try to identify the source of light in a painting because I know that artists often use light to reveal what they want the viewer to see. When looking at this painting, it would be easy to assume that the light is coming from behind, from the windows through which we see a Renaissance landscape. But the source of light in this painting actually is the face of Jesus reflecting on all of the disciples but Judas, who is underpainted with black and denied a brightened countenance.

The source of light points to what anchors the painting: the presence of Jesus. This is emphasized by the use of perspective, a Renaissance invention used to create an illusion of three-dimensionality in a two-dimensional space. The windows and other architectural elements create lines that end up in a single point, called the "vanishing point." In *The Last Supper*, the vanishing point ends on the forehead of Jesus, the centerpiece of the painting. But if the painting were an equilibrium centered on Jesus, it would not create the psychological tension we feel from it. The tension is there because Philip breaks up the visual stasis.

Philip's body gets flattened in any reproduction or photograph (see plate B, *The Last Supper* with perspective added) of the painting. However, a trained artist or viewer looking at the actual piece can see that Philip's body is contorted, surrounded by negative spaces. The angle compresses his body and accentuates the movement of his reaction. Leonardo's genius used the vanishing point not only to anchor the painting but also to create waves of motion that shock us into shedding visual conventions.

If you are an artist working on a large commission, you know that looking up at a painting distorts what you paint, so you account for that by exaggerating the vertical. In other words, you make the figure taller than it needs to be. What I noticed looking up at *The Last Supper* is that Leonardo did not make Philip's body taller but instead kept his body twisted, compressed, and angular. That is why in reproductions of this painting Philip's body does not stand out.

If Leonardo did not elongate the figure, why does Philip stand out when you stand under the painting?

It took me the entire fifteen minutes that I was allowed in Santa Maria delle Grazie to understand what Leonardo did. And then the whole painting began to open up to me. In a true visual code, Leonardo reveals both his genius and the true message of the painting.

Philip stands out because he visually breaks the horizontal plane. The top of Philip's head aligns itself with the perspective lines parallel to the windows. The eye attends to his head, magnetically drawn to the perspective line that juts out from the horizontal line. This happens only if you are standing below the painting. Another figure breaks the horizontal line, which is accentuated by the head of Jesus, and that other figure is Judas. *The Last Supper* is to be read from Philip to Judas, through the body of Christ, creating several visual *v*'s and *w*'s.

In the New Testament, Philip is one of the Seven,[2] the closest disciples of Christ. It's possible that he knew Jesus and his family and may have grown up with Jesus. Philip is also noted in Scripture for having the ability to point others to Christ. He convinced Nathanael to "come and see" Christ in the first chapter of the Gospels, and in the book of Acts (the historical document of the early church) he continues to draw many to Jesus, including the Ethiopian eunuch who was found reading the prophecy of Isaiah in Gaza.[3]

It is clear to me that of the four Gospels, John is the one Leonardo relied on the most. Matthew reads like a legal case to clearly convict Judas of betrayal. Both Luke and Mark seem to focus on Peter, his betrayal compared to Judas, and his eventual restoration to become the founder of the early church. But John records in detail what Leonardo depicted, from John's reclining figure to Judas's darkness, from Thomas's infamous skepticism to Philip's surprise at what Jesus' mouth had just uttered.

Leonardo was interested in one thing: the psychological depiction of a night of betrayal. John 14:8 records Philip asking a question that reverberates throughout the painting:

> Philip said, "Lord, show us the Father and that will be enough for us."
>
> Jesus answered: "Don't you know me, Philip, even after I have been among you such a long time? Anyone who has seen me has seen the Father. . . . Believe me when I say that I am in the Father and the Father is in me; or at least believe on the evidence of the miracles themselves. I tell you the truth, anyone who has faith in me will do what I have been doing. He will do even greater things than these, because I am going to the Father." (verses 8-9,11-12)

Philip asked for evidence, a question that must have also filled Leonardo's mind. Philip's comment is one of near frustration, an insider's exasperation, and therefore even the nature of his request assumes a close, trusting relationship. Jesus responded to the core of Philip's question by saying, "Don't you know me, Philip?" In doing so, Jesus made one of the most remarkable promises ever made to his followers (more on this later).

It makes sense, then, that when Jesus revealed that he was to be betrayed by a close friend, Philip leaped out of his chair in disbelief. A pronouncement of betrayal most shocks the trusted. To this innocence Leonardo gives the most weight, initiating a shock wave that reverberates throughout the painting and the corridors of time.

Betrayal has always defined our lives, and since ancient times artists have given ample attention to this common human experience, in forms like Greek tragedies and Shakespearian plays. But today we live in the expectation of one betrayal after another, of relationships breaking up or of another political or religious leader found in scandal. As we read tabloid accounts of celebrity comings and goings, we simultaneously bemoan and are bemused by their depth of woes.

Our culture of betrayal goes way beyond individual failures; it is a culture that has lost the belief in the good, the true, and the beautiful. Without the a priori conscience that believes in civilization's own integrity—that wrong can be righted and that creativity is a gift to society—no art, and no work of our hands, can be infused with a transcendent vision. The culture of betrayal denies the potential to hope and is determined to quickly self-destruct.

Our galleries and contemporary museums (not to mention our movie theaters and bookstores) are full of such vacuous images, but blaming artists is not helpful. Rather it is more accurate to say that artists are simply reacting to and honestly recording the conditions of the culture. "The power of the arts to anticipate future social and technological developments, by a generation and more, has long been recognized. In this century Ezra Pound called the artist the antennae of the race," stated Marshal McLuhan, twentieth-century media ecologist.[4] Artists are "a canary in the cultural mines."[5]

Artists smell the poisoned air and sing.

But Leonardo was born in a different time. He was given the legacy of Giotto and Fra Angelico. He had patronage that he could count on from the church and from powerful individuals who also assumed a certain worldview. He had geniuses as contemporaries, including Michelangelo and Botticelli, who also worked from a convention that assumed a direct connection between culture and beauty, goodness and truth.

In a sense, there was an innocence from which the artists of the time could work, but it was not naïveté. Leonardo was not naive, and he was certainly a religious skeptic. But this commission, only one of two wall commissions he received, gave him an opportunity to work out of the metanarrative (the gospel story) with conviction and force. He could trust that his paintings were meant to last and speak to the generations to come. Because of corruption within the church, of which Leonardo was certainly aware and decried in his notes, and because of the loss of patronage about to ensue, this assumption saw its zenith in *The Last Supper*.

We may never recover such innocence again. In our current culture of betrayal we need evermore to see and stand under *The Last Supper*. We need to seriously consider "receiving" the message, as C. S. Lewis suggested, and allowing the work to speak into our lives.

In *The Da Vinci Code*, the character Robert Langdon, a professor of symbology, finds it significant that Jesus and the effeminate figure seated on his right form the letter *m*. Moreover, Langdon believes this second figure is not Saint John but Mary Magdalene, the "bride of Christ," dressed as a man.

Yes, there is an *m* imbedded in the painting, but the novel does not go far enough in tracing its mystery.

The real *m* or series of *m*'s, starting from Philip's outstretched hand, do not end with John but with Judas. More specifically, the shock wave ends in Judas's right hand, which holds the moneybag, symbolically depicting the very coins that Judas would receive for betraying Jesus.

Is the figure of John effeminate? Yes. But every male figure that Leonardo painted bordered on androgyny. Leonardo's depiction of the sexual genre has never been a secret, and even a critique of such in open forums would not have surprised Leonardo. What would be shocking to him is the viewer's somehow not recognizing the greatest message imbedded in the painting—that Judas, the seed of betrayal, *is in all of us*.

Most of the paintings of the Last Supper from Leonardo's era depict Judas leaving the room. Yet Leonardo made a radical decision to keep Judas as part of the "inner circle," placing him—and, by association, us—at the table. Judas is depicted explicitly as part of the inner circle of the disciples and sits directly in front of Peter, who Christ identified as the "rock" of the early church. Like Philip, Leonardo wanted to point to a deeper journey. And when we stand under this genius work, we too take part in that journey.

The Da Vinci Code phenomenon is not about conspiracy theories; it is a symptom of our cultural ills, of how easily we accept distortion and betrayal as normative and necessary. We are trained to cheapen our dialogue to fit our darkened realities.

Today our moneybags are full of flashy, counterfeit sound bites.

Christians must understand that this can easily happen in our worship as well as in popular culture. We want God to be palatable and to fit our needs and realities so we don't have to practice a daily discipline. I venture to say that what goes on inside our worship services has a great impact upon the larger cultural condition. Could it be that the reason we have such a divided nation, insistent on quick judgment, is because the church does not fully know how to live and exercise grace? Could it be that the reason we do not have a culture full of beauty is because our worship is not beautiful? Could it be that the cause of our shortened attention span in contemporary society is because the church has not trained us to listen well?

In our culture of betrayal, we are quick to impose our own views on layers of established systems. Thus, even a work of art is to be distrusted. Rather than trying to "under-stand" the work, we stand over it and dismiss it as unreadable. Or worse yet, we impose a critical ideology upon it without first allowing the work to affect us.

In doing so we miss out on experiencing what the work of art can offer, and consequently we do not journey into the power of genuine art. This lack of authentic encounters leads only to a vortex of distrust, fueled by the media, whose capital is fear. We are drowning in a deluge of despair, and our memories of the good, the true, and the beautiful have nearly faded completely.

Sadly, today no one has Leonardo's ability or skill to ask complex and deeply layered cross-disciplinary questions in his or her art, even with the advent of moving images. It may be argued that Leonardo was the last painter to have the ability to integrate history, theology, science, and art with such mastery. Consider this: *Can we think of any other artist after Leonardo whose work would be a target for an intriguing conspiracy tale?* No one has had the genius, the psychological complexity, or the level of skill and patronage, not even Picasso, van Gogh, or Warhol. Don't get me wrong; there are certainly notable contributors, such as Grünewald, Caravaggio,

Rembrandt, Gorky, and Kandinsky, but none of these artists has had the enormous social influence, not just in the arts but in all human endeavors—such as art, sciences, philosophy, engineering, music—that Leonardo has had.

Our wrestling against an established system demands that the system has strength enough to withstand the challenge and at the very least serve as a dialectical opponent. The center must hold in order for the surface tension to break. Thus, even in facile intrigue there is always substance underneath. Our critique of contemporary culture must begin with that assumption. And then we must not just engage and critique from that conviction; we must create out of that center.

To Leonardo, such a foundation was immediately accessible. In order to paint as he did, he had to be convinced of a center that holds.

So who is at the center? Where does the vanishing point end?

It ends on the forehead of the Savior.

And that foundation will hold, no matter how full our moneybags get or how little it takes for us to engage in betrayal. To Leonardo, the triangular shape of Jesus literally holds the painting in its visual movement. To Leonardo, that foundation was never in question; to him it was a question of evidence.

Jesus exhorted Philip to believe based on the evidence of miracles. Leonardo, of all people, wanted evidence. He looked for it in the stars and sketched it in the sinews of cadavers. He sought resolution in the core of his creativity and asked deeply phenomenological and existential questions. In other words, Leonardo saw himself at the table too, and he saw himself leaping up like Philip at the comment of Jesus. Even as a skeptic, Leonardo was at once in a deep, creative engagement with the Savior, and he approached God with intellectual rigor and dialogue.

In this remarkable passage of John 14, Jesus, the miracle worker, tells his disciples, in direct answer to Philip's comments, that they shall do the "greater work":

> I tell you the truth, anyone who has faith in me will do what
> I have been doing. He will do even greater things than these,
> because I am going to the Father. (verse 12)

What were the "greater things" to which Jesus referred? What could be greater than raising Lazarus from the dead, an event recorded in John 11?

Leonardo framed the answer implicitly in *The Last Supper* with Philip's earlier words: "Come and see."

The greater things were in telling the world to "come and see." Come and see a masterpiece to consider these eternal questions. And that is what Leonardo determined to undertake in *The Last Supper*.

The Last Supper may even miraculously outlast celluloid (or even digital) and our fifteen-minutes-of-fame mind-set as the world deteriorates in front of our eyes. *The Last Supper*, in that sense, is a perfect complement, or even an antidote, for the twenty-first-century cultural landscape, exposing us for who we truly are. Even in a mere fifteen-minute encounter, the work leaves us spellbound for a moment of wonderment.

This is why we all need to travel to Milan, just for a momentary decompression, to stand under Christ, who is about to reach for that bread of Communion. Like Leonardo, we may even desire to participate in that evening, in the suffering of the One and only true Artist, and follow him to the vanishing point, the source of our bright countenance.

There, witnessing the earthy vermillion glow of the Milan rooftops, we may find ourselves deeply reflecting on the gospel of John, chapter 14, where the Savior's still voice continues to expose the depth of our woes and the secrets of our depravity. In Christ's outstretched arms, we may yet find our malaise lifted and our imaginations sparked to do greater things.[6]

August 2006

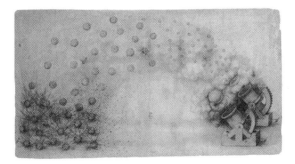

Shrapnel-Mortar, Leonardo da Vinci sketch.

XXIII

Operation Homecoming: Epistles of Injury

I recently found myself at New York's Symphony Space, listening to the voices of soldiers. As a National Council on the Arts member, I was representing the National Endowment for the Arts for the release of the book *Operation Homecoming* (Random House, edited by Andrew Carroll). The NEA created *Operation Homecoming* in order to give returning soldiers from Afghanistan and Iraq an opportunity to write down their wartime experiences. The program conducted workshops led by Pulitzer-winning Vietnam-era writers to help the troops tell their stories. On that night of celebration, with actors highlighting the evening (Matthew Modine, Joan Allen, and, most memorably, Stephen Lang), as I sat next to one of the soldier/writers, I had a strange and uncomfortable revelation: a revelation that surely had been bubbling up in me in recent years. How much of the world's art and literature is linked to wartime experiences?

The writings of soldiers, or writings about wars in general, have indeed defined our literature and the arts, from Homer to Dante to Hemingway. If you removed works of art that do not in some way relate to or respond to wars, our cultural landscape would be full of holes (think of Picasso's great masterpiece of Spain's civil war, *Guernica*). Perhaps that's what Jesus meant when he warned us "such things [wars] must happen" (Matthew 24:6). He did not validate wars by saying this, but he wanted to make sure we understood the inevitability of them: that our inner malaise will surely be translated into greater conflicts. But to have the Prince of Peace tell us that wars *must* happen is more than troubling. Must we be haunted by wars as part of God's plan of redemption? Must art exist as primarily funerary?

In modern times, Rothko, Mondrian, and other twentieth-century painters wove the horrors of the atomic age into their work as if to visit Hiroshima over and over again. Both working abstractly, Rothko gave that post-atomic glow an ethereal transcendence even as Mondrian stubbornly, and valiantly, insisted on the order of grids against the approaching chaos. In both cases, they were exiled to New York because of the dark specters of evil marching into their homelands. Surrealism (as the MOMA/National Gallery exhibit showed) screamed against the insanity of fear birthed in the trenches of World War I. These artists are often remembered for their antipatriotic rants or, at best, for being ambivalent observers and most definitely antiestablishment. Ironically, they are now seen as the establishment in the institutions of museums and academia. But the best of the arts still can rise above the institutions and establishment that gave permission for them or the conflicts that they escaped. The arts speak into a void, creating a moment of clarity, a pause in the frenzy.

Then there are the J. R. R. Tolkiens and C. S. Lewises of the world, whose front-line experiences gave birth to the most resonant, faith-filled literature of our last century. Tolkien imagined through the dark trenches, surrounded by dying friends, and chose to speak directly against his own fear by naming characters and places of imagined reality that would later form the basis for *The Lord of the Rings*. Lewis, too, injured in the war, later recounted that his journey from atheism to faith was paved by his sense of loss, by the inconsolable violation ("the problem of pain," he called it) that he felt in his bones. Going through such horrors is no guarantee of a recovery of faith, but it does suggest that faith and culture are linked to the crisis that surrounds us.

T. S. Eliot would have found this dialogue not so unfamiliar. His wartime journey to write *The Waste Land* could also describe our survey of Darfur and Afghanistan.

In the *Four Quartets*, he described "the unimaginable Zero Summer" of the atomic devastation, but he ended with hope in the "still point of the turning world," producing a rare articulation of the heart's navigation from fear to love. But today, in the shadows of our current chaos in Iraq and with the bullet holes in an Amish school still fresh in our minds, such sentiment can come across as too optimistic and even unkind.

I read recently that most of early Christian art (at least the examples that have survived) were funerary in nature. Apparently, even in the world of faith, art is obsessed with death. Surely, it would be the darkest of confessions for any artist working today to admit that his or her visions are driven by the haunts of war and death and that, like Dante, imaginative reality is filled with a vision of purgatory. On the contrary, our recent contemporary art scene is rushing to escapism, lacking in engagement with the present darkness and even the disciplined skill to describe the horror. Such a confessional would seem welcome in today's climate of super-ficiality. Pausing to listen to the writings of soldiers in *Operation Homecoming*, though, I have begun to glimpse a new kind of realism.

These men and women chose to write while staring into the abyss: to record both their fears and hopes in this time of certain chaos. They grieve over lost lives and opportunities, but they also speak well of their pets and ordinary sunlit days. Theirs is a stark realism: observing the life surrounding the turmoil, wrestling against the fading memories of loved ones, comrades, and the stenches of war. So many of *Operation Homecoming*'s pages are filled with e-mails, which, similar to radio dispatches, will remain deeply etched in our minds as immediately potent. These voices are directed toward our private spheres but now allowed to be made public. They deserve our hushed attention for their honest grappling with inner turmoil. Their accounts are true survivor tales, but without any shred of sensation-alism. Told sometimes gingerly, sometimes in expletives, after a while, the stories seem to dwell in my consciousness as these soldiers become my imaginary neighbors, people whom I might encounter on my street or kick a soccer ball around with. I am surprised at how much humor fills these pages—not the sanitized kind but the raw, grimy kind that belongs in beer halls and late-night comedy shows. Refreshingly free of showmanship in our glitz-filled cultural universe, these writings serve more than to recount the war; they speak into our lives with authenticity and remind us somehow that, despite it all, humanity can still reign in a cruel kaleidoscope of fear called war.

There are poignant lessons, of a soldier writing home as he flew over Iraq, a geography lesson that spans some three thousand years. "Have you heard of Mesopotamia?" wrote Lieutenant Colonel Cohoes to his sons. "Two great rivers of the world, the Tigris and the Euphrates, flow together here then empty into the Persian Gulf. . . . King Nebuchadnezzar (I can't say it either) built the hanging Gardens of Babylon about 2,600 years ago."[1] Of course, in the reading that took place at Symphony Space, Matthew Modine could not pronounce Nebuchadnezzar either.

A soldier of Korean descent recounted his adoptive American father and grandfather fighting in *their* wars. Echoed throughout the book is generational lineage to wars; it is not an isolated experience to one generation. Christy De'on Miller, a divorced mom and soldier, mourns the loss of her only son Aaron. In an essay she called "Timeless," she wrote:

> At times I believe I can learn to live a life without my son.
> After all, I must. I am certain there are other mothers who have
> lost their boys—car accidents, war, illness—who can shop for
> dinner at the local grocer's without the macaroni-and-cheese
> boxes suddenly causing them grief. Moms who can roll sausage
> balls without tears; perhaps the festive food would even cause a
> smile. But the memory of him is planted in everything around
> me. Inside of me. So much is gone. Him, of course. But so
> much of him has been lost, is fading, breaking down. His blan-
> ket, his watch, his uniform.[2]

The writings amplify the details of life—not just theirs, but ours. They let us into the writers' worlds, to share in their grief, their loss, and their confusion.

After listening to account after account of Afghan and Iraqi soldiers and their families, here was another revelation: I too live in a war zone. A different, milder version for sure, sanitized and better packaged. Photos of the bright new facades of "you can have it all" condominiums, to be completed in 2010, try to convince us that we are all better in downtown Manhattan. Their airbrushed architectural renderings are what a friend calls "architectural porn." But, nevertheless, I live and raise my family in a place called Ground Zero, and reading *Operation Homecoming* opened my eyes to see the invisible collateral of a war far away, shadowing us everywhere.

However, there *are* visible scars in culture. The battle is about the imaginative territories of hope against fears, the sacrifice of love against a misplaced devotion, the anger of revenge against forgiveness. It is a battle that rages in the minds of our youth as they negotiate the labyrinth of a techno-frenzied universe, sharing a communion of broken promises. When the manifestation of such collateral damage ambushes us, like in the pastoral Amish landscapes recently, or in Littleton, Colorado, in 1998, in a high school named after a delicate wild flower, we are astonished.

When the evil struck the sleepy Amish community near Lancaster—when a milkman-turned-gunman systematically shot girls one by one—there was a hidden story. John Hewett, the former development director of the NEA, who also happens to be an ordained minister, called it "A Miracle Nobody Noticed." He noted in a sermon he gave:

> I'm convinced most of us get through most days without think-
> ing about God much. I was having one of those days a few
> weeks ago, until I heard about Marian and Barbie Fisher, two of
> the ten girls in the West Nickel Mines Amish School. Marian,
> the oldest, was 13. Her sister Barbie, who lived, is 11. When it
> became obvious what was about to happen that ghastly morning,
> Marian turned to the killer and said, "Shoot me and leave the
> other ones loose." "Shoot me next," Barbie said. "Shoot me next."
> Two children willing to lay down their lives for their friends.
> Wonder where they got an idea like that? That's another miracle
> nobody noticed. [3]

Perhaps a new renaissance will be birthed out of the "mouths of babes" like these: "Shoot me and leave the other ones loose." Or it may flow out of a grieving mother and soldier, like De'on grieving for Aaron, a Marine who lost his life protecting his wounded comrades. Perhaps we will see that whether we are soldiers or housewives or Pulitzer Prize–winning writers (or all of the above), we need to realize that we are not home, at least not yet. That's the only faith that can compel us to say, "Shoot me." The girl did not complain that "this is unfair" or argue "this is unjust." She just said, "Shoot me."

Such fragile but heroic voices in the face of violence can easily be ignored, inaudible to our doomed ears. It certainly did nothing to stop a milkman from unloading his anger by pulling the trigger. Perhaps such otherworldly gestures look as pathetic, or beautiful, as the string quartet that played on as the *Titanic* sank. But I submit to you that here, in a miracle nobody noticed, is a bugle call also directed toward us artists. It begins in a belief that we are to live our lives for others. Art should let "the other ones loose" from the bondage of decay, apathy, and loss. To the extent we are able to do that, we will see a new language of expression that is not self-centered but self-giving and generous. Yes, I believe that art can, and ought to, exist apart from wars. But the only place in history where this has been the case—a place called Eden, where a poet named Adam dwelled—is today hidden inaccessibly beneath the rubble of Iraq.

Operation Homecoming gives us authentic voices that seek to be responsible stewards of their experiences. Why would that simple gesture seem so foreign and refreshing? Has our culture become so cynical that we no longer have the capacity to listen without having a wry, critical distance? Or has the media become so profit-driven and sensationalistic that it can no longer mediate information responsibly? The soldiers faced certain death and stood over the rubble that might have crushed them, but having lived, they owned the experience and chose to tell the tale artfully and carefully. If we all live in a war zone of some kind, should we not do the same? Words alone can impregnate promise or despair in such a precipice; the arts can inspire or despise humanity.

In Jesus' realism of "such things must happen," he was also reminding us that our sacrifice, either for just or unjust reasons, would not be the last word. Our efforts, however noble, will not end the cause of injustice. Nevertheless, we are all called to self-sacrifice. None is exempt, not even a pacifist thirteen-year-old secluded as far away from Iraq as humanly possible. And Jesus knows, firsthand, what it means to die an unjust death without picking up a stone or a spear. Instead, he continues to breathe life into us in our funerary songs. By listening to these soldiers and poets, we may even begin to feel that life-breath, a hint of a culture of self-giving. Despite the anguish, De'on wrote with the same quiet surrender of the Amish sisters:

> My faith doesn't equal that of Job's. I question. Why has God cut the fruit from my vine? Taken the only child that remained? Left me with no hope for a grandchild? I'm certain there can be no more. No more children.
>
> And yet I have no particular animosity for my son's killer. He's a nameless and faceless combatant to me. Should I ever have the opportunity to meet him, I hope that I'd forgive him. To me, the buck stops with the Father. His power stings at times. But He's listened to me; perhaps He's even cried with me. And yes, I do know what I'm talking about here. *It's a belief, man.* Aaron's words. *You either believe in God or you don't.* Yes, I'd forgive. I do forgive. There is absolutely nothing I'd do to keep myself from spending eternity with God and Aaron.[4]

Our path back to Eden is blocked, but there is a way in to the feast of the selfless. Only the words of forgiveness, utterly stripped down to the core of faith, can echo the timeless, or the timeful,[5] promise of an Easter morning. That is our true homecoming. Even if the condition is unbearably chaotic or simply cruel, these authentic voices refract in our fear-dominated cultural landscape, mediating how we can choose to face a new day and breathing certain hope into our stricken hearts.

December 2006

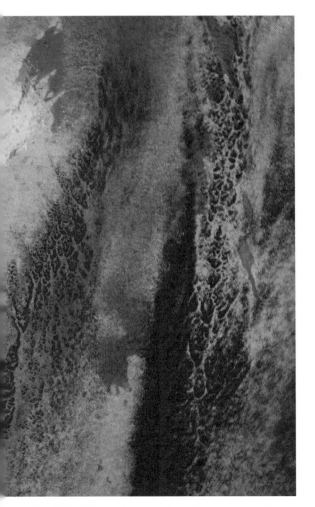

Cascade Wings, 2008 photo by Makoto Fujimura of a work in progress. Original
piece is done with mineral pigments on Kumohada paper.

Postscript

As I reedited *Refractions*, and in some cases rewrote the essays extensively, I now see that my writing process very much parallels my painting process. These layers of thoughts and ideas need to refract like the prismatic minerals that I use in painting. The editing process is akin to washing away some parts of the painting to reveal more subtle refractions, and rewriting can change the whole essay without losing the thread of the original.

I've noted that *Refractions* is not merely the title of the book but a whole underlying philosophical framework for creativity and life that I've been developing. I now realize I have been unconsciously expanding this theoretical and theological grid as I wrote these essays, not only to describe the creative process, but also to develop a communication style suited for my temperament and to advocate for community vision for the church, to honor artists, and even to argue for democratic ideals.

In my paintings, each prismatic grain of sand captures light, and layers allow color to resonate, and our eyes delight in seeing multiple shards of light scattered upon the surface. Our eyes capture more than what our minds can comprehend and catalog. A viewer needs time to begin to trust her vision, to truly *see* the surface of the painting. Words, in my opinion, have similar quality and power. But rather than using the senses to take in refractions with our eyes, written words can have the gripping power of resonation in our memories and can begin to affect the intuitive, giving us maps of future imaginative journeys.

I suppose being a semi-abstract painter, I need words to complement and even refract with visual imagery. Thus, like William Blake, my greatest inspiration from the Romantic age who created etchings filled with words and imagery, I do not see these essays as separate from my visual works. Like Blake, I paint and write not to argue for certain ideology, but I desire to journey with the creative Spirit, to bring light to the gospel of Jesus Christ, whose words and actions refract via eternity, bringing his prismatic light into our broken realities.

May such mediated light shine upon the church to steward culture and creativity, to love the arts, so that we may be more effective ambassadors for the gospel of Jesus Christ, the Author of Creativity.

Notes

Makoto Fujimura's art is represented by Dillon Gallery, New York.

Introduction

1. The highest public arts position in the United States. National Council on the Arts members are appointed by the president and approved by the Senate. Past members include Leonard Bernstein, Richard Diebenkorn, Duke Ellington, Helen Hayes, Charlton Heston, Harper Lee, Gregory Peck, Sidney Poitier, David Smith, John Steinbeck, and Isaac Stern.
2. International Arts Movement began in Japan in 1991. It is a nonprofit arts advocacy group whose mission is to "gather artists and creative catalysts to wrestle with the deep questions of art, faith, and humanity in order to inspire the creative community to engage the culture that is and create the world that ought to be." www.internationalartsmovement.com
3. NEA Jazz Master's Award, New York Hilton, January 2004.
4. See Nat Hentoff's excellent discussion of the ideals of democracy reflected in the history and music of jazz. Read, for instance, *Jazz: New Perspectives on the History of Jazz by Twelve of the World's* (reprint of the 1959 ed. published by Rinehart, New York).
5. Leo Tolstoy, *What Is Art and Essays on Art* (Oxford: Oxford Press, 1930), 286.
6. Tolstoy, 288.
7. The Village Church (Presbyterian Church in America) is a daughter church of Redeemer Presbyterian Church and began in 1994 in Greenwich Village.

Chapter 1: *A Second Wind*

1. I want to thank Dr. Tim Keller for suggesting the use of this term at an IAM lecture in SoHo in 1998.
2. William Blake, "Auguries of Innocence."

Chapter 2: *Splendor*

1. See Makoto Fujimura, *River Grace* (Poiema Press, International Arts Movement publication, 2007), www.rivergrace.com for more detailed description of Nihonga and my testimonial of coming to faith.
2. Makoto Fujimura, *River Grace* (Poiema Press, International Arts Movement publication, 2007), 6.
3. I recently lectured in China, and I was told by a Chinese art professor that these three Nihonga masters are considered to be "three pillars" there as well.
4. Pieter Bruegel the Elder (about 1525–1569) is generally considered the greatest Flemish painter of the sixteenth century.
5. Nishijin design, developed for court nobles of Kyoto, stems from fifth-century Japan.
6. Matazo Kayama, *Infinite Space*, trans. Makoto Fujimura (Tokyo: Shogakukan Press, 1994), 54.
7. See cover of *River Grace* (www.rivergrace.com).

Chapter 3: *Bert's Disappearing Weather Maps*

1. See Ono no Komachi's tanka, for instance.

Chapter 4: *A Parable of Roots (Beijing Journal)*

1. The UK developer of Oxford Place who commissioned the painting.

Chapter 5: *The Disintegration Loops: September 11th Issue*

1. http://www.mmlxii.com.
2. http://www.tribecatemporary.com.
3. http://www.pitchforkmedia.com/record-reviews/b/basinski_william/disintegration-loops.shtml.
4. See Romans 8.
5. See Genesis 2:19.
6. Genesis 2:19.
7. 2 Corinthians 4:16.

Chapter 6: *Fallen Towers and the Art of Tea*

1. Laurie Fendrich, "Point of View: History Overcomes Stories," *The Chronicle of Higher Education*, September 28, 2001, http://chronicle.com/free/v48/i05/05b02001.htm.
2. Takashi Murakami has become one of the most celebrated pop artists of our time.

3. *ShinGeijutsu Shinjun Magazine*, November 2001, Tokyo, translation, 9.
4. Laurie Fendrich, "Point of View: History Overcomes Stories," *The Chronicle of Higher Education*, September 28, 2001, http://chronicle.com/free/v48/i05/05b02001.htm.
5. F. Scott Fitzgerald, quoted in Ric Burns and James Sanders, *New York: An Illustrated History* (New York: Knopf, 1999), 386.
6. Luke 13:1-5.
7. Quoted by Rev. Clyde Godwin in reference to Jerry Sittser, *A Grace Disguised* (Grand Rapids, MI: Zondervan, 1995).
8. Tomonobu Imamichi, "Poetry and Ideas," *Doyo Bijutsu Magazine* 2, no. 114 (1994): 42.
9. Originally published by *Image Journal*, no. 32 (Fall 2001).

Chapter 7: *Nagasaki Koi Voting Booth*

1. Gwenda Blair, "Designers Redefine the Political Machine," *New York Times*, October 7, 2004.
2. See the essay on Christo and Jean-Claude, highly regarded public art creators of our day, on page 91.
3. American architect and set designer.

Chapter 8: *"L.I.B.E.S.K.I.N.D."*

1. Daniel Libeskind, *Breaking Ground* (New York: Riverhead Books, 2004), 43.
2. During a private interview with Daniel Libeskind for IAM Conference, 2007, see www.iamny.org for mp3 download of Libeskind's interview with Dick Staub.
3. Libeskind, 43.
4. Libeskind, 44.
5. Libeskind, 44.
6. *The Wall Street Journal* article by critic Ada Louise Huxtable.
7. http://www.gothamgazette.com/iotw/chosen/tour8.shtml.
8. See Chapter 10, *Breaking Ground,* for his account of how David Childs, the architect most critical of Libeskind's use of 1,776 feet as a symbol of freedom, ended up somehow using the concept for his design of the Freedom Tower.
9. Libeskind, 288.

Chapter 10: *Dances for Life*

1. See C. S. Lewis, *The Weight of Glory* (New York: Touchstone, 1996), 25.
2. Hans Rookmaaker, *Art Needs No Justification*, chapter 2 (Downers Grove, IL: InterVarsity, 1978), http://www.dickstaub.com/culturewatch .php?record_id=912.
3. CIVA conference, Montreal, 1997. I was sitting next to him at a panel discussion when he made this most poetic/theological remark.

Chapter 11: *Surfacing Dolphins*

1. James Elkins, *Why Art Cannot Be Taught* (Champaign, IL: University of Illinois Press, 2001), 189–190.
2. For an excellent discussion on poststructuralism, see Donald D. Palmer, *Structuralism and Poststructuralism for Beginners* (Danbury, CT: Forbeginnersbooks, 2006).
3. William Blake, *Jerusalem*, chapter 2, plate 31.

Chapter 12: *A Visual River of Gold*

1. http://www.geocities.com/Yosemite/9173/umbrellas.html.

Chapter 13: *Finding Neverland*

1. http://www.geocities.co.jp/Hollywood-Miyuki/4222/films/04/findingneverland.htm, the original quote is no longer available, translation mine.
2. I want to acknowledge Professor William Edgar, Westminster Seminary, for this definition of entertainment.

Chapter 15: *Gretchen's Butterflies*

1. Roberta Smith, "Gretchen Bender, 53, an Artist Working in Film and Video, Dies," *New York Times*, December 24, 2004, http://www.nytimes.com/2004/12/24/arts/24bend.html.
2. http://www.hihowareyou.com.
3. Elaine Scarry, *On Beauty and Being Just* (Princeton: Princeton University Press, 1999), 31.

Chapter 16: *Why Art?*

1. http://www.unausa.org.
2. Aylmer Maude, *The Life of Tolstoy Later Years* (Whitefish, MT: Kessinger Publishing, 2007), appendix 1.
3. The account of book *She Said Yes* by Misty Bernall (Rifton, NY: The Plough Publishing House, 1999), detailing the confession of Cassie Bernall, has been disputed. See http://books.google.com/books?id=JujrCCedbicC&pg=PA121&lpg=PA121&dq=controversy+over+columbine+testimony&source=web&ots=Dr7bPA1CX0&sig=vPWi6p9q-IEUe4LUZYa9QVNyz7c. Despite the uncertainty of what was exactly said, Cassie Bernall's testimony and her willingness for die for her faith are clear as noted in her diaries.

Chapter 17: *Optimal Foraging Theory: Can You Have Your Birds and Eat Them Too?*

1. http://www.birds.cornell.edu/ivory/#.
2. James Gorman, "In the Swamp, an 'Extinct' Woodpecker Lives," *New York Times*, May 3, 2005, http://www.nytimes.com/2005/04/29/science/29bird.html.

3. See Tyson's core values statements: http://www.tysonfoodsinc.com/corporate/info/mission.asp.

4. John James Audubon (April 26, 1785 – January 27, 1851) was an American ornithologist, naturalist, hunter, and painter. His paintings are extraordinary for their aesthetic presence as much as they are known for ornithological records.

Chapter 18: *Planting Seedlings in Stone: Art in New York City*

1. An Armenian-born American painter whose studio at Union Square, New York City, in the 1930s had a profound effect on the development of abstract Expressionism.

2. A Latvian-born Jewish American painter and printmaker who also emigrated to New York City in the early twentieth century. One of my greatest influences in considering the metaphysical possibilities of paintings.

3. Author of *The Reenchantment of Art* and *Conversations Before the End of Time*, Gablik boldly challenged the assumptions behind modernism in her work, paving the way for consideration of beauty and relational aesthetics in the current art world.

4. Suzi Gablik, "The Nature of Beauty in Contemporary Art," *New Renaissance*, 8, no. 1 (1998). http://www.ru.org/81gablik.html. She quotes Sandra Chia, an Italian contemporary artist.

5. Essay originally written for *Comment* magazine, December 2, 2005, https://wrf.ca/comment/article.cfm?ID=151.

Chapter 19: *Walking Backward into the Future*

1. Many people assume that Japanese blood is homogenous, but history tells us that the first capital of Nara was as diverse culturally and racially as Queens, New York.

2. Paul Elie, *The Life You Save May Be Your Own* (New York: Farrar, Straus and Giroux, 2003), 13–14.

3. Thomas C. Oden, *After Modernity . . . What?* (Grand Rapids, MI: Zondervan, 1990), 43.

Chapter 20: *The Housewife That Could*

1. Douglas Martin, "Jane Jacobs, Social Critic Who Redefined and Championed Cities, Is Dead at 89, *New York Times*, April 26, 2006, Arts, http://www.nytimes.com/2006/04/26/books/26jacobs.html?scp=1&sq=April+26%2C+2006+Jane+Jacobs&st=nyt.

2. Jane Jacobs, interviewed by Jim Kunstler for *Metropolis Magazine*, March 2001, http://www.kunstler.com/mags_jacobs.htm.

3. http://www.kunstler.com/mags_jacobs.htm.

4. Now former director, as Jeff heads up his own urban design firm in Washington, DC. See his lecture as part of IAM's Gathering, 2008, at www.iamny.org.

Chapter 21: *Fra Angelico and the Five-Hundred-Year Question*

1. The first entry of the following website is Baghdad being "sacked." Found at http://en.wikipedia.org/wiki/Battle_of_Baghdad_(1258).
2. Francis did this by rehumanizing the process of communicating the gospel into the core essence of life, leading his followers to summarize his approach with a famed quote (though apparently not a direct quote of Francis, but a summary): "Preach the gospel at all times. Use words if necessary."
3. http://www.metmuseum.org/special/Fra_Angelico/images.asp.
4. See Richard J. Mouw's excellent book *When the Kings Come Marching In: Isaiah and the New Jerusalem* (Grand Rapids, MI: Eerdmans, 2002) for further illumination on this subject.
5. See Genesis 2; Isaiah 60; 1 Corinthians 3; Revelation 21.

Chapter 22: *Come and See: Leonardo da Vinci's Philip in* The Last Supper

1. C. S. Lewis, *An Experiment in Criticism* (Cambridge: Cambridge University Press, 1992), 18–19.
2. Luke 6:14-16 states, "Simon (whom he named Peter) and his brother Andrew, James, John, Philip, Bartholomew, Matthew, Thomas, James son of Alphaeus, Simon who was called the Zealot, Judas son of James, and Judas Iscariot, who became a traitor." Traditionally, Peter, Andrew, James, John, Philip, Matthew, and Thomas are considered to be the Seven. In *The Last Supper*, James Major sits closer to Philip than Matthew.
3. Acts 8:26-40.
4. Marshall McLuhan and Lewis H. Lapham, *Understanding Media* (Cambridge: MIT Press, 1994), xi.
5. Elsewhere, I have attributed this quote to Marshall McLuhan, but it may be my own metaphorical extension of what he states in *Understanding Media*.
6. A special thanks to Dr. John E. Walford of Wheaton College and Dr. William A. Dyrness of Fuller Seminary for their insights to prepare for this essay.

Chapter 23: *Operation Homecoming: Epistles of Injury*

1. Andrew Carroll, ed., *Operation Homecoming* (New York: Random House, 2006), 232.
2. Carroll, 245.
3. John Hewett, "A Miracle Nobody Noticed," text e-mailed to the author on November 17, 2007.
4. Carroll, 245.
5. I want to thank Dr. Tim Keller for suggesting the use of this term at an IAM lecture in SoHo in 1998.

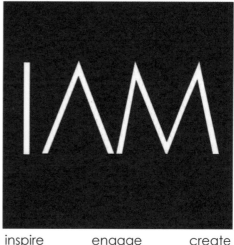